ISBN: 9781313271219

Published by:
HardPress Publishing
8345 NW 66TH ST #2561
MIAMI FL 33166-2626

Email: info@hardpress.net
Web: http://www.hardpress.net

THE JOURNAL OF
SUBMARINE COMMANDER
VON FORSTNER

PASSENGERS AND CREW LEAVING A SINKING LINER TORPEDOED BY A GERMAN
SUBMARINE IN THE MEDITERRANEAN

THE JOURNAL OF SUBMARINE COMMANDER VON FORSTNER

TRANSLATED BY
MRS. RUSSELL CODMAN

WITH AN INTRODUCTION BY
JOHN HAYS HAMMOND, Jr.

TOUT BIEN OU RIEN

BOSTON AND NEW YORK
HOUGHTON MIFFLIN COMPANY
The Riverside Press Cambridge
1917

CONTENTS

ILLUSTRATIONS

FOREWORD

THE following pages form an abridged translation of a book published in 1916 by Freiherrn von Forstner, commander of the first German U-boat. It was written with the somewhat careless haste of a man who took advantage of disconnected moments of leisure, and these moments were evidently subject to abrupt and prolonged interruptions. Many repetitions and trivial incidents have been omitted in this translation; but, in order to express the personality of the Author, the rendering has been as literal as possible, and it shows the strange mixture of sentimentality and ferocity peculiar to the psychology of the Germans.

FOREWORD

Part of the book gives a technical description,—not so much of the construction of a submarine as of the nature of its activities,—which presents us an unusual opportunity to glean a few valuable facts from this personal and intimate account of a German U-boat. We are inclined to a certain grim humor in borrowing the candid information given to us Americans so unconsciously by Freiherrn von Forstner, for he could hardly suppose it would fall into the hands of those who would join the fighting ranks of the *hated enemy*, as, in his bitter animosity, he invariably calls the English whenever he refers to them.

Several chapters in this book are simple narratives of the commander's own adventures during the present naval warfare waged against commerce.

His attempts at a lighter vein often provoke a smile at the quality of his wit, but he is not lacking in fine and manly virtues. He is a loyal comrade; a good officer concerned for the welfare of his crew. He is even kindly to his captives when he finds they are docile victims. He is also willing to credit his adversary with pluck and courage. He is never sparing of his own person, and shows admirable endurance under pressure of intense work and great responsibility. He is full of enthusiastic love for his profession, and in describing a storm at sea his rather monotonous style of writing suddenly rises to eloquence. But in his exalted devotion to the Almighty War Lord, and to the Fatherland, he openly reveals his fanatical joy in the nefarious work he has to perform.

FOREWORD

It is difficult to realize that this ardent worship of detail, and this marvelous efficiency in the conservation of every resource, are applied to a weapon of destruction which directs its indiscriminate attacks against women and children, hospital transports, and relief ships. Nothing at the present day has aroused such fear as this invisible enemy, nor has anything outraged the civilized world like the tragedies caused by the German submarines.

This small volume may offer new suggestions to those familiar with the science of submarine construction, and it may also shed a little light, even for lay readers, on a subject which for the last three years has taken a preëminent place in the history of the War.

INTRODUCTION

THE CHALLENGE TO NAVAL SUPREMACY

I

IN a letter to William Pitt, of January 6, 1806, relating to his invention of a submersible boat, Robert Fulton wrote prophetically, "Now, in this business, I will not disguise that I have full confidence in the power which I possess, which is no less than to be the means, should I think proper, of giving to the world a system which must of necessity sweep all military marines from the ocean, by giving the weaker maritime powers advantages over the stronger, which the stronger cannot prevent."

INTRODUCTION

It is interesting to note that, about a hundred years later, Vice-Admiral Fournier of the French Navy stated before a Parliamentary committee of investigation that, if France had possessed a sufficient number of submersibles, and had disposed them strategically about her coasts and the coasts of her possessions, these vessels could have controlled the trade routes of the world. He said also that the fighting value of a sufficient number of submersibles would reëstablish the balance of power between England and France.

The history of naval warfare during the last few months has confirmed the opinions of these two authorities, although in a manner which they in no way anticipated.

Direct comparison is the usual method by which the human mind estimates values. We would measure the strength of two men by pitting them against each other in physical encounter; in the same way, we are prone to measure the combative effect of weapons by pitting them in conflict against other weapons. But modern warfare is of so complex a nature that direct comparisons fail, and only a careful analysis of military experience determines the potentiality of a weapon and its influence on warfare. Robert Fulton and Admiral Fournier both indicated that they believed in the submersible's supremacy in actual encounter with capital ships. The war, so far, has shown that, in action between fleets, the submersible has played a negative part. In the Jutland Bank battle, the submersible, handicapped in speed and eyesight, took as active a part, as a Jack Tar humorously put it, "as a turtle might in a cat fight." Not even under the extraordinary conditions of the bombardment in the Dardanelles, when the circumstances were such as lent themselves strikingly to submarine attack, did these vessels score against the fleet in action.[1]

It is easy to understand why the submersible did not take a vital part in any of the major naval actions. In the naval battle of to-day we have a number of very high-speed armored craft fighting against one another over ranges extending up to 17,000 yards. There is a constant evolution in the position of the ships which it is impossible to follow from the low point

[1] The "Majestic" was torpedoed at the Dardanelles, while at anchor. The "Triumph" was torpedoed while moving slowly; both warships had out their torpedo nets.

of vantage of a periscope, for the different formations of ships mean nothing to the submersible commander. He is so placed that his range of vision is extremely limited, and, on account of the low speed of his boat while submerged, he can operate over only a very limited area of water while the other vessels are moving many miles. Then, too, he is extremely vulnerable to the effect of enemy shells and to the ramming of enemy ships. Under these conditions the submersible commander is more or less forced to a policy of lying ambushed to surprise his enemy. It is said that the " Lusitania " was decoyed into a nest of submersibles. There was but little chance of torpedoing her in any other way. There is also the statement that Admiral Beatty passed with his battle-cruisers through a flotilla of enemy submersibles without being touched.

Submersibles cannot attack their target in definite formations as do surface vessels, and therefore they cannot operate in numbers with the same effectiveness as do the latter. They must maneuver more or less singly, and at random. Being limited to the torpedo, which, when they are submerged, is their sole weapon of attack, they have an uncertain means of striking their armed enemy. The eccentricities of the automobile torpedo are well known; but, even eliminating the fact that this missile is unreliable, the important question of accuracy in the estimate of range and speed which the submersible commander has to make before firing the torpedo must be considered. There is usually a large percentage of error in his calculations unless the submersible is extremely close to its target. Realizing these limitations, the German submersibles are equipped with small torpedoes, which are generally fired at ranges not exceeding eight hundred to two thousand yards. The necessity of approaching the target so closely is, of course, a tremendous handicap in the general operation of these boats. In view of these facts, it is not surprising that the submersible should not have been able to sweep the capital ship from the seas, as was predicted by certain experts before the war.

II

Admiral Sir Cyprian Bridge regards the functions of defense by a navy as divisible into three main classifications. He says, "The above-mentioned three divisions are called in common speech, coast defense, colonial defense, and defense of commerce." From this classification we are given a hint as to what a sailor means by "naval supremacy," "freedom of the seas," and other terms so misused that to-day they mean nothing. "Coast defense" means defense against invasion; "colonial defense" means the safeguarding of distant possessions against enemy forces; the "defense of commerce" means such supremacy on the seas as will insure absolute safety of the mercantile marine from enemy commerce-destroyers.

To-day every great nation is waging a trade war. The industrial competition of peace is as keen as the competition of war. All the great Powers realized years ago that, to gain and keep their "place in the sun," it was necessary for them to construct navies that would insure to them a certain control of the seas for the protection of their commerce. In this way began the abnormal naval construction in which the Powers have vied with one another for supremacy.

A simple way of looking at the question, what constitutes the power of a fleet, is to consider the warship as merely a floating gun-platform. Even though this floating platform is the most complex piece of mechanism that was ever contrived by man, nevertheless its general function is simple. The war has given us enough experience to convince us that the backbone of a navy is, after all, the heavily armored ship of moderately high speed, carrying a very heavy armament. This floating gun-platform is the structure best fitted to carry large guns into battle, and to withstand the terrific punishment of the enemy's fire.

The battleship is to-day, notwithstanding the development of other types, queen of the seas. It is therefore not difficult to estimate the relative power of the fleets of different nations. In fact, a purely engineering estimate of this kind can be made, and the respective ranks of the world's naval powers ascertained. Germany has shown all through the war that she thoroughly appreciated the British naval supremacy. Her fleet has ventured little more than sporadic operations from the well-fortified bases behind Heligoland. It was probably the pressure of public opinion, and not the expectation that she would achieve anything of military advantage, that forced her to send her high-sea fleet into conflict with the British squadrons off Jutland.

If one should examine the course of this battle, which has been represented by lines graphically showing the paths of the British and German fleets, one

ERRATUM

In Introduction, page xxi, line 6 from the bottom, for "1915" read "1916."

literally herded on May 31, 1915, from 5:36 in the afternoon until 9 o'clock that night. Admiral von Scheer, however, fought the only action which it was possible for him to fight. It was a losing action, and one which he knew, ship of moderately high speed, carrying a very heavy armament. This floating gun-platform is the structure best fitted to carry large guns into battle, and to withstand the terrific punishment of the enemy's fire.

The battleship is to-day, notwithstanding the development of other types, queen of the seas. It is therefore not difficult to estimate the relative power of the fleets of differ-

——— ——— ——— ——— the war that she thoroughly appreciated the British naval supremacy. Her fleet has ventured little more than sporadic operations from the well-fortified bases behind Heligoland. It was probably the pressure of public opinion, and not the expectation that she would achieve anything of military advantage, that forced her to send her high-sea fleet into conflict with the British squadrons off Jutland.

If one should examine the course of this battle, which has been represented by lines graphically showing the paths of the British and German fleets, one could easily see how the British imposed their will upon the Germans in every turn that these lines make. It reminds one very much of the herding of sheep, for the German fleet was literally herded on May 31, 1915, from 5:36 in the afternoon until 9 o'clock that night. Admiral von Scheer, however, fought the only action which it was possible for him to fight. It was a losing action, and one which he knew,

from a purely mathematical considera-
tion, could not be successful.

Through the very definiteness of this
understanding of what constitutes
naval strength, Great Britain's navy
until recently has remained a great
potential force, becoming dynamic for
only a few hours at Jutland, after
which it returned to that mysterious
northern base whence it seems to
dominate the seas. Because of the
potentiality of these hidden warships,
thousands of vessels have traversed
the ocean, freighted with countless
tons of cargoes and millions of men
for the Allies. Even at that psycho-
logical moment when the first hundred
thousand were being transported to
France, Germany refrained from a
naval attack which might have turned
the whole land campaign in her favor.

To-day, however, the world is awakening to a new idea of sea-power, to a new conception that will have a far-reaching influence on the future development of naval machinery.

Sir Cyprian Bridge has stated that one of the functions of a fleet is the defense of commerce. There is no more important function for a fleet than this. A nation may be subjugated by direct invasion, or it may be isolated from the world by blockade. If the blockade be sufficiently long, and effectively maintained, it will ruin the nation as effectually as direct invasion.

Thus, in the maintenance of a nation's merchant marine on the high seas, its navy exercises one of its most vital functions. There can, therefore, be no naval supremacy for a nation unless its commerce is assured of immunity from considerable losses through the attack of its enemy. It is idle for us to speak of our naval supremacy over Germany, when our navies are failing in one of their most important functions, and when our commerce is suffering such serious losses. The persons best qualified to judge are those who are most anxious regarding the present losses in mercantile tonnage.

While it has been shown that the submersible of to-day, as a fighting machine, is considerably limited, and in no sense endangers the existence of the capital ship, nevertheless in the new huge submersible it seems that the ideal commerce-destroyer has been found. This vessel possesses the necessary cruising radius to operate over

sufficient distances to control important routes; it makes a surface speed
great enough to run down cargo steamers, and has a superstructure to mount
guns of considerable power (up to six-
inch). It embodies almost all the quali-
fications of the light surface cruiser,
with the additional tremendous advantage of being able to hide by
submergence. To be completely successful, it must operate in flotillas
of hundreds in waters that are opaque
to aërial observation. Germany has
but a limited number of these submersibles, otherwise she would be able
to crush the Allied commerce.

The ideal submersible commerce-
raider should be a vessel of such displacement that she could carry a
sufficient number of large guns in her
superstructure to enable her to fight off

the attack of surface destroyers and the smaller patrol craft.[1] She should be capable of cruising over a large radius at high speed, both on the surface and submerged. The supersubmersible flotillas should comprise fifty or sixty of these units. The attack on the trade routes should be made by a number of flotillas operating at different points at unexpected times. Today Germany has concentrated her submarine war particularly in the constricted waters about England. It is here that the shipping is most congested, and therefore the harvest is richest, but it is also easier to protect the trade routes over these limited areas of water by patrols, nets, etc., than it would be to protect the entire

[1] The Germans have in operation submersibles of 2000 tons displacement.

trans-oceanic length of the steamship lanes. If the submersible were capable of dealing directly with the destroyer in gun-fighting, a tremendous revolution would take place in the tactics of "submarine swatting." Then it would be difficult to see how the submersible could be dealt with.

Improvement in motive machinery is the vital necessity in the development of the submersible. The next few years may see unexpected strides taken in this direction. A great deal will also be accomplished in perfecting methods of receiving sounds under water, particularly in relation to ascertaining the direction of these sounds. When this is done, it will be possible for the submersible commander to tell a great deal about the positions of the vessels above him, and thus his artificial ears will compensate to a great extent for his blindness. By the addition of a greater number of torpedo-tubes, and the improvement of their centralized control in the hand of the commander at the periscope, along lines which we are now developing, it will be possible for the submersible to achieve a greater effectiveness in its torpedo fire. Probably torpedoes will then be used only against the more important enemy units, such as battleships, cruisers, and the like. To be certain of striking these valuable targets would be worth expending a number of torpedoes in salvo fire.

Whether the German U-boat campaign succeeds or not will be largely a question of the number of submersibles that the Central Powers can put into service, and to what extent the submersible will be developed during the present war.

III '

German submarines have sunk over 7,250,000 tons of the Allied shipping. In December, 1916, it was stated in the British Parliament that the merchant marine of Great Britain had at that time over 20,000,000 tons. Within the first three months of the unrestricted submarine warfare, 1,100,000 tons of British shipping went to the bottom. At this rate, England would lose 25 per cent of her merchant marine per annum. It is for this reason that the attention of the entire world is concentrated upon the vital problem of the submarine menace. On land, the Central Powers are still holding their ground, but there is a continuous increase of the forces of the Allies which should lead finally to such a preponderance of power as will overwhelm the forces opposed to them. The Allied armies, however, depend for their sustenance and supplies upon the freedom of the seas. The trade routes of the world constitute the arteries which feed the muscles of these armies. Germany is endeavoring to cut these arteries by the submarine. Should she even appreciably limit the supplies that cross the ocean to the Allies, she will bring about a condition that will make it impossible to augment their armies. In this way there will inevitably be a deadlock, which, from the German standpoint, would be a highly desirable consummation.

Obviously, the first method of handling the submarine problem would be to bottle the German undersea craft in their bases. There has been a number of proposals as to how best to accomplish this. It has been stated that the English Navy has planted mines in channels leading from Zeebrugge and other submarine bases; but it is necessary only to recall the exploits of the E-11 and the E-14 of the British Navy at the Dardanelles, to see that it would not be impossible for the Germans to pass in their U-boats through these mine-fields into the open sea. It will be remembered that the E-11 and the E-14 passed through five or more mine-fields, thence through the Dardanelles into the Sea of Marmora, and even into the Bosphorus under seemingly impossible conditions. Yet, in spite of the tremendous risks that they ran, these boats continued their operations for some time, passing up as far as Constantinople, actually shelling the city, sinking transports, and accomplishing other feats which have been graphically described in the stories of Rudyard Kipling. And again, if the mine-fields were placed in close proximity to their bases, it would be comparatively easy for German submersibles of the Lake type, possessing appliances to enable divers to pass outboard when the vessel is submerged, to go out and cut away the mines and thus render them ineffective.

Nets are also used to hinder the outward passage of the submarine. These nets can likewise be attacked and easily cut by devices with which modern U-boats are equipped. The problem of placing these obstacles is a difficult one, in view of the fact that the ships so engaged are harassed by German destroyers and other enemy craft. Outside of Zeebrugge, shallow water extends to a distance of about five miles from the coast, and it has been suggested that a large number of aircraft, carrying bombs and torpedoes, should be used to patrol systematically the channel leading from that port to deep water, with the intent of attacking the submersibles as they emerge from this base. It is ridiculous to suppose that the Germans would not be able to concentrate an equally large number of aircraft, to be supported also by anti-aircraft guns on the decks of destroyers and by the coast defenses. We have not yet won the supremacy of the air, and it must inevitably be misleading to base any proposition on the assumption that we are masters of that element.

The problem of bottling up the submersibles is enormously difficult, because it necessitates operations in the enemy's territory, where he would possess the superiority of power. I believe that the question of operations against the submarine bases is not a naval but a military one, and one which would be best solved by the advance of the Western left flank of the Allied armies.

The second method is to attack the submarines with every appliance that science can produce. In order to attack the submarine directly with any weapon, it is necessary first to locate it. This is a problem presenting the greatest difficulty, for it is by their elusiveness that the submarines have gained such importance in their war on trade. They attack the more or less helpless merchant ships, and vanish before the armed patrols appear on the scene.

Almost every suitable appliance known to physics has been proposed for the solution of the problem of submarine location and detection. As the submarine is a huge vessel built of metal, it might be supposed that such a contrivance as the Hughes induction balance might be employed to locate it. The Hughes balance is a device which is extremely sensitive to the presence of minute metallic masses in relatively close proximity to certain parts of the apparatus. Unfortunately, on account of the presence of the saline sea-water, the submersible is practically shielded by a conducting medium in which are set up eddy currents. Although the sea-water may lack somewhat in conductivity, it compensates for this by its volume. For this reason, the induction balance has proved a failure.

But another method of detecting the position of a metallic mass is by the use of the magnetometer. This device operates on the principle of magnetic attraction, and in laboratories on stable foundations it is extremely sensitive. But the instability of the ship on which it would be necessary to carry this instrument would render it impossible to obtain a sufficient degree of sensitiveness in the apparatus to give it any value. The fact that the submersible is propelled under water by powerful electric motors begets the idea that the electrical disturbances therein might be detected by highly sensitive detectors of feeble electrical oscillations. The sea-water, in this case, will be found to absorb to a tremendous extent the effects of the electrical disturbance. Moreover, the metallic hull of the submersible forms in itself an almost ideal shield to screen the outgoing effect of these motors.

Considerable and important development has been made in the creation of sensitive sound-receiving devices, to hear the propeller vibrations and the mechanical vibrations that are present in a submersible, both of which are transmitted through the water. There are three principal obstacles to the successful use of such a device: when the submersible is submerged, she employs rotary and not reciprocating prime-movers, being in consequence relatively quiet when running under water, and inaudible at any considerable distance; the noises of the vessel carrying the listening devices are difficult to exclude, as are also the noises of the sea, which are multitudinous; finally, the sound-receiving instruments are not highly directive, hence are not of great assistance in determining the position of the object from which they are receiving sounds.[1]

To locate the submersible, aërial observation has been found useful. It is particularly so when the waters are clear enough to observe the vessel when submerged to some depth, but its value is less than might be supposed in the waters about the British Isles

[1] Big strides, however, have been made lately in overcoming these shortcomings, and it would appear that the principle of sound-detection is the most hopeful one for us to follow.

and Northern Europe, where there is a great deal of matter in suspension which makes the sea unusually opaque. The submersible, however, when running along the surface with only its periscope showing, is more easily detected by aircraft than by a surface vessel. Behind the periscope, there is a characteristic small wake, which is distinguishable from above, but practically invisible from a low level of observation. Many sea-planes are operating on the other side for the purpose of locating enemy submersibles and reporting their presence to the surface patrol craft. In order to overcome the disadvantages of creating the periscope wake which I have mentioned, it is reported that the Germans have developed special means to allow the U-boats, when raiding, to submerge to a fixed depth without moving. To maintain any body in a fluid medium in a static position is a difficult matter, as is shown in the instability of aircraft. One of the great problems of the submersible has been to master the difficulties of its control while maintaining a desired depth. The modern submersible usually forces itself under water, while still in a slightly buoyant condition, by its propellers and by the action of two sets of rudders, or hydroplanes, which are arranged along its superstructure and which tend to force it below the surface when they are given a certain inclination; but should the engines stop, the diving rudders, or hydroplanes, would become ineffective, and, because of the reserve buoyancy in the hull, the vessel would come to the surface.

INTRODUCTION

In order to maintain the vessel in a state of suspension under water without moving, it would be necessary to hold an extremely delicate balance between the weight of the submarine and that of the water which it displaces. Variations in weights are so important to the submersible that, as fuel is used, water is allowed to enter certain tanks to compensate exactly for the loss of the weight of the fuel. To obtain such an equilibrium, an automatic device controlled by the pressure of the water, which, of course, varies with the depth, is used. This device controls the pumps which fill or empty the ballast-tanks, so as to keep the relation of the submersible to the water which it displaces constant, under which condition the vessel maintains a fixed depth. The principle of this mechanism is, of course, old, and was first embodied in the Whitehead torpedo, which has a device that can be set so as to maintain the depth at which it will run practically constant. With the addition of a telescopic periscope, which can be shortened or extended at will, it will be possible for the U-boat to lie motionless with only the minute surface of the periscope revealing her position.

IV

To attack the submersible is a matter of opportunity. It is only when one is caught operating on the surface, or is forced to the surface by becoming entangled in nets, that the patrol has the chance to fire upon it. Against this method of attack, modern submersibles have been improving their defenses. To-day, they are shielded with armor of some weight on the superstructure and over part of the hull. They are also equipped with guns up to five inches in diameter, and, affording, as they do, a fairly steady base, they can outmatch in gun-play any of the lighter patrol boats which they may encounter.

One of the important improvements which have been made has resulted in the increased speed with which they now submerge from the condition of surface trim. A submersible of a thousand tons displacement will carry about five hundred tons of water ballast. The problem of submerging is mainly that of being able rapidly to fill the tanks. On account of the necessity of dealing with large quantities of water in the ballast system, the European submersibles are equipped with pumps which can handle eight tons of water per minute.

Again, the speed which the electrical propulsion system gives the vessel on the surface greatly increases the pressure which the diving rudders can exert in forcing the submersible under water. This effect may be so marked that it becomes excessive, and Sueter emphasizes the point that vessels at high speed, when moving under water, may, on account of the momentum attained, submerge to excessive depths. To eliminate this tendency, there is a hydrostatic safety system which automatically causes the discharge of water from the ballast-tank when dangerous pressures are reached, thus bringing the submersible to a higher level where the pressure on the hull will not be so severe. From this it follows that the

INTERIOR OF A SUBMARINE

opportunity of ramming a submersible, or of sinking it by gunfire, is greatly minimized, since the vessel can disappear so rapidly.

A great deal has been attempted with nets. Fixed nets extend across many of the bodies of water around the British Isles. Their positions, doubtless, are now very well known to the Germans. The problem of cutting through them is not a difficult one. Moreover, the hull of the submersible has been modified so that the propellers are almost entirely shielded and incased in such a way that they will not foul the lines of a net. There has also been a steel hawser strung from the bow across the highest point of the vessel to the stern, so that the submersible can underrun a net without entangling the superstructure. Some nets are towed by surface vessels. The process is necessarily slow, and to be effective the surface vessel must know the exact location of the submersible. Towing torpedoes or high explosive charges behind moving vessels has been developed by the Italian Navy, but the chances of hitting a submersible with such devices are not very great.

Bomb-dropping from aëroplanes can be practiced successfully under exceptional conditions only. In view of the fact that such bomb-dropping is exceedingly inaccurate, and that the charges carried are relatively small, this form of attack ordinarily would not be very dangerous for the submersible. Surface craft have also employed large charges of high explosives, which are caused to detonate by hydrostatic pistons upon reaching a certain depth. Patrol boats carry such charges in order to overrun the submersible, drop the charges in its vicinity, and by the pressure of the underwater explosion crush its hull. Since the pressure of an underwater explosion diminishes rapidly as the distance increases from the point of detonation, it would be necessary to place the explosive charge fairly close to the hull of the submersible to be certain of its destruction. To accomplish this, it would seem that the ideal combination would be the control of an explosive carrier by radio energy directly from an aëroplane. Thus we would have a large explosive charge under water where it can most effectively injure the submersible, controlled by the guidance of an observer in the position best suited to watch the movements of the submerged target.

The third method by which to frustrate the attack of the submersible is to give better protection to the merchant marine itself. While a great deal of ingenuity is being concentrated on the problem of thwarting the submersible, but little common sense has been used. While endeavoring to devise intricate and ingenious mechanisms to sink the submersible, we overlook the simplest safeguards for our merchant vessels. To-day, the construction of the average ship is designed to conform to the insurance requirements. This does not mean in any way that the ship is so constructed as to be truly safe. Thousands of vessels that are plying the seas to-day are equipped with bulkheads that are absolutely useless because they do not extend high enough to prevent the water from running from one part of the ship to another when the ship is partially submerged. Then again, the pumping system is so arranged as to reach the water in the lower part of the hull when the ship is up by the head. Should the ship be injured in the forward part and sink by the head, these pumps would be unable to reach the incoming water before her condition had become desperate. There is a vessel operating from New York to-day worth approximately a million dollars, and if she were equipped with suitable pumps, which would cost about a thousand dollars, her safety would be increased about forty per cent. Her owners, however, prefer running the risk of losing her to expending a thousand dollars! If the merchant vessels were made more torpedo-proof, it would be an important discouragement to the U-boat commander. During the past two years of the war, nineteen battleships have been torpedoed, and out of this number only three have been sunk, showing that it is possible by proper construction to improve the hull of a ship to such an extent that it is almost torpedo-proof. While it may not be practicable, on account of the cost, to build merchant vessels along the lines of armed ships, nevertheless much could be done to improve their structural strength and safety; and since speed is an essential factor in circumventing torpedo attack, new cargo-carriers should be constructed to be as fast as is feasible.

So radically have conditions changed

that to-day we have a superabundance of useless dreadnaught power. The smaller guns of some of these vessels, and their gun crews, would be far more useful on the merchant vessels than awaiting the far-off day when the German fleet shall venture forth again. The submersible must be driven below the surface by a superiority of gunfire on the part of the merchant marine and its patrols. In this way the submersible would be dependent upon the torpedo alone, a weapon of distinct limitations. In order to use it effectively, the submersible must be not more than from eight hundred to two thousand yards from its target, and must run submerged at reduced speed, thus greatly lessening its potentiality for destruction. To-day, submersibles are actually running down and destroying merchant vessels by gunfire. If merchant vessels carried two high-speed patrol launches equipped with three-inch guns of the Davis non-recoil type, and these vessels were lowered in the danger zone as a convoy to the ship, such a scheme would greatly lessen the enormous task of the present patrol. In the event of gunfire attack by a submersible, three vessels would be on the alert to answer her fire instead of one: an important factor in discouraging submersibles from surface attack!

The future of the submarine campaign is of vital importance. The prospect is not very cheerful. Laubeuf states that at the beginning of the war Germany had not over thirty-eight submersibles. This statement may be taken with a grain of salt; the Germans do not advertise what they have. It is probable, however, that to-day they have not more than two hundred submersibles in operation. Over four thousand patrol boats are operating against this relatively small number, and yet sinkings continue at an alarming rate. It is estimated that Germany will be able to produce a thousand submersibles in the coming year and man these vessels with crews from her blockaded ships. This will be a tremendous addition to the number she has now in operation. The greater the number of submersibles she has in action, the greater the area the submarine campaign will cover. The number of patrol vessels will have to be increased in direct proportion to the area of the submarine zone. Since a large number of patrol boats has to operate against each submersible, it will be seen that a tremendous fleet will have to be placed in commission to offset a thousand submersibles. Thus the problem becomes increasingly difficult, and the protection of the trade route will be no more thoroughly effected than it is to-day — unless we overwhelm the enemy by a tremendous fleet of destroyers.

THE JOURNAL OF SUBMARINE COMMANDER VAN FORSTNER

I

ORDERED TO COMMAND A SUBMARINE

EVERY year about the first of October, at the time of the great army maneuvers, new appointments are also made in the navy; but, unlike our army brothers, who from beginning to end remain permanently either in the artillery, cavalry, or infantry, we officers of the navy are shifted from cruiser to torpedo boat, from the ship of the line to the hated office desk on land at the Admiralty, in order to fit us to serve our Almighty War Lord in every capacity and to the best advantage. The commander of a torpedo boat must be familiar with the service on board a dreadnaught or on any other large ship, for only those who are intimately acquainted with the kind of ship they are going to attack possess sufficient skill to destroy it.

For the first time in the autumn of 190– some of us were surprised at the announcement: "Ordered on board a submarine." This order naturally met with an immediate response, but it brought a new outlook on the possibilities of our career, for we had not yet been trained to this branch of the service which our Almighty War Lord had only recently added to the Imperial Navy. The question was, should we be able to perform this new duty?

It is well known that the French were the first to complete a type of submarine navigable underseas, and the English unwillingly, but with a sly anticipation of coming events, copied this type of boat.

To all outward appearance we kept aloof from following the example of our neighbors, and our chiefs of the Admiralty were beset with expostulations on the subject, but they were silently biding their time while our enemies of to-day were bragging about their successful experiments with their newly constructed submarines. To the dismay and astonishment of our opponents it was only when the right hour had struck that our navy revealed that it had similar weapons at its command; it therefore prepared for them some disagreeable surprises, and set its special seal from the very beginning on the maritime warfare.

3

I remember a talk I had with an old army officer a few years ago, when I had just received my appointment to a submarine. We were speaking of U-boats and aëroplanes, and he exclaimed: "Ach! my dear Forstner, give it up! The bottom of the ocean is for fishes, and the sky is for birds."

What would have happened to us in this war had we not so proudly excelled above the earth and beneath the sea?

At first a mystery still veiled our knowledge concerning our submarines; we were told that the dear, good, old U-boat No. 1 had splendidly stood every test, and shortly after, in October, 190–, I went on board, and had the honor later to command her for two years. But during this period, for several years, the greatest secrecy surrounded this new weapon of our navy;

strictest orders were given to admit no one on board, not even high officers; only admirals were allowed to penetrate within, and on every matter concerning our U-boats we had to maintain absolute silence. Now, however, that our usefulness has been so fully justified, the veil of discretion can be somewhat lifted, and I can describe within certain limits the life and activities on board a submarine.

II

BREATHING AND LIVING CONDITIONS UNDER WATER

A SUBMARINE conceals within its small compass the most concentrated technical disposition known in the art of mechanical construction, especially so in the spaces reserved for the steering gear of the boat and for the manipulation of its weapons.

The life on board becomes such a matter of habit that we can peacefully sleep at great depths under the sea, while the noise is distinctly heard of the propellers of the enemy's ships, hunting for us overhead; for water is an excellent sound conductor, and conveys from a long distance the approach of a steamer. We are often asked, "How can you breathe under water?" The health of our crew is the best proof that this is fully possible. We possessed as fellow passengers a dozen guinea pigs, the gift of a kindly and anxious friend, who had been told these little creatures were very sensitive to the ill effects of a vitiated atmosphere. They flourished in our midst and proved amusing companions.

It is essential before a U-boat submerges to drive out the exhausted air through powerful ventilating machines, and to suck in the purest air obtainable; but often in war time one is obliged to dive with the emanations of cooking, machine oil, and the breath of the crew still permeating the atmosphere, for it is of the utmost importance to the success of a submarine attack that the enemy should not detect our presence;

therefore, it is impossible at such short notice to clear the air within the boat. These conditions, however, are bearable, although one must be constantly on the watch to supply in time fresh ventilation.

Notwithstanding certain assertions in the press of alleged discoveries to supply new sources of air, the actual amount remains unchanged from the moment of submersion, and there is no possibility, either through ventilators or any other device so far known in U-boat construction, to draw in fresh air under water; this air, however, can be purified from the carbonic acid gas exhalations by releasing the necessary proportion of oxygen. If the carbonic acid gas increases in excess proportion then it produces well-known symptoms, in a different degree, in different in-

8

dividuals, such as extreme fatigue and violent headaches. Under such conditions the crew would be unable to perform the strenuous maneuver demanded of it, and the carbonic acid must be withdrawn and oxygen admitted.

The ventilation system of the entire submarine is connected with certain chemicals, through which the air circulates, whose property is to absorb and retain the carbonic acid. Preparations of potassium are usually employed for this purpose. Simultaneously, cylinders of oxygen, under fairly high pressure, spray oxygen into the ventilation system, which is released in a measure proportionate to the number of the crew; there is a meter in the distributing section of the oxygen tubes, which is set to act automatically

9

at a certain ratio per man. The ordinary atmosphere is bearable for a long time and this costly method of cleansing the air is used only as a last resort; the moment at which it must be employed is closely calculated to correspond, not only with the atmospheric conditions at the time of submersion, but also to the cubic quantity of air apportioned to each man according to his activities and according to the size of the boat.

It is unnecessary to clear the air artificially during a short submersion, but during prolonged ones it is advisable to begin doing so at an early hour to prevent the carbonic acid gas from gaining a disproportionate percentage, as it becomes then more difficult to control, and it is obvious that it is impossible to dissipate the fumes of cooking, the odors of the machine oil, and the breath of the crew.

Taken altogether one can live comfortably underseas, although there is a certain discomfort from the ever-increasing warmth produced by the working of the electrical machinery, and from the condensation created by the high temperature on the surface of the boat plunged in cold water, which is more noticeable in winter and in colder regions.

It is interesting to observe that the occupations of the crew determine the atmospheric conditions: the quantity of air required by a human body depends entirely on its activity. A man working hard absorbs in an hour eighty-five liters of air. Besides the commander, who is vigorously engaged in the turret, — as will be hereafter described,

— the men, employed on the lateral and depth steering, and those handling the torpedo tubes, are doing hard physical work. The inactive men use up a far smaller quantity of air, and it is ascertained that a man asleep requires hourly only fifteen liters of air. A well-drilled crew, off duty, is therefore expected to sleep at once, undisturbed by the noise around them, and their efficiency is all the greater when the time comes to relieve their weary comrades. We had a wireless operator on board whose duties ceased after submersion, and he had so well perfected the art of sleeping that he never cost us more than fifteen liters of air, hourly, underseas.

The length of time that a U-boat can remain under water depends, as we stated above, on the atmospheric conditions at the moment of plunging, and on the amount of oxygen and chemicals taken on board. We can stay submerged for several days, and a longer period will probably never be necessary.

The distance of vision varies somewhat under water, as we look out from the side windows cut into the steel armor of the commander's conning tower. We can naturally see farther in the clear water of the deep ocean than in the turbid, dirty water at the mouth of a river, and the surface of the water-bottom has a direct influence on the sight, which is far more distinct over a light sand than over dark seaweed or black rocks, and at an upper level the sunshine is noticeable many meters under water. But in any case, the vision underseas is of the shortest, and does not extend beyond a few meters; light objects and even the stem and stern of our own boat are invisible from the turret. We are unaware, therefore, of advancing ships, derelicts, or projecting rocks, and no lookout can preserve us from these dangers.

The crew is entirely ignorant of their surroundings. Only the commander in his turret surveys through the periscope now and then a small sector of the horizon; and in turning round the periscope he gradually perceives the entire horizon. But this survey demands great physical exertion, which on a long cruise is most fatiguing. The periscopes erected through the upper cover of the turret must not be too easily turned in their sockets, and the latter are very tightly screwed in, for otherwise they would not be able to resist the water pressure at a great depth. The effort of simply turning the periscope is so exhausting that casual observations of the horizon are made by the officer of the watch; but during naval maneuvers or in time of war, the commander alone manipulates the periscope. It is essential in this case that the periscope should not arise needlessly above water and betray the presence of the U-boat.

The commander must possess the absolute confidence of his crew, for their lives are in his hands. In this small and carefully selected company, each man, from the commanding officer down to the sailor boy and down to the stoker, knows that each one is serving in his own appointed place, and they perform their duties serenely and efficiently.

I have always allowed every man on board once, in turn, to have a look through the periscope; it is their highest ambition, and the result is excellent, for it reassures them and they feel more confident as to their own safety after the granting of this small favor.

As we advance underseas, unless passing through a school of fish, we seldom see any fish, for the noise of the propellers frightens them away; but when we lie at rest on the bottom of the ocean, the electric lights allure them, and they come and stare at us with goggling eyes close to the windows in the turret.

The life, therefore, in our "cylinder" as we call it, offers a good deal of variety. The term "cylinder" is exact, for the inner conformation of a submarine is necessarily rounded, so that relatively thin partitions can successfully resist the greatest pressure of water.

III

SUBMERSION AND TORPEDO FIRE

A NEW passenger, for the first time in a submarine, has often professed to be unaware that he was fathoms deep under water and has been quite unconscious that the boat had been diving. Of course his astonishment indicates that he was not in the compartment where these maneuvers take place, for it is in the commander's turret that the whole apparatus is centralized for submersion, for steering to the right depth, and also for emersion. At this juncture every man must be at his post, and each one of the thirty members of the crew must feel individually responsible for the

17

safety of the whole in the difficult and rapid maneuver of plunging, for the slightest mistake may endanger the security of the boat.

The central control, situated in the commander's turret, is in reality the brain of the boat. When the alarm signal is heard to change the course from surface navigation to subsurface navigation, several previously designated members of the crew take their post of duty in the commander's turret. The commander, himself, is on duty during the whole of the expedition in time of war, and he seldom gets a chance for rest in his tiny little cabin. Day and night, if there is the slightest suspicion of the approach of the enemy, he watches on the exposed bridge on the top of the turret; for a few seconds' delay in submerging might forfeit the taking of a much coveted prize. So he learns to do without sleep, or to catch a few brief seconds of repose by lying down in his wet clothes, and he is at once ready to respond to the alarm signal of the officer of the watch.

In one bound he is once more surveying the horizon through the periscope, or mounts to the bridge to determine with his powerful field glass whether friend or foe is in sight. His observations must be taken in the space of a few seconds, for the enemy is also constantly on the lookout, and continual practice enables the sailor in the crow's nest to detect the slender stem of a periscope, although the hull of the boat is scarcely visible on the face of the waters.

The commander must come to a

prompt decision as soon as he locates the adversary's exact position. Not only may a retarded submersion spoil our plan of attack, but we are exposed to being rammed by a rapidly advancing steamer; our haste must be all the greater if the conditions of visibility are impaired, as is often the case on the high seas, for it takes time for the U-boat to submerge completely, and during this process it is helplessly exposed to the fire of long distance guns.

Calmly, but with great decision, the commander gives the general orders to submerge. The internal combustion engines, the oil motors which, during surface navigation are used to accelerate the speed of the boat, are immediately disconnected, as they consume too much air underseas, and electric motors are now quickly attached and set in motion. They are supplied by a large storage battery, which consumes no air and forms the motive power during subsurface navigation. Of course electricity might be employed above water, but it uses up much current which is far more expensive than oil, and would be wasted too rapidly if not economized with care.

It would be convenient to employ the same oil motor for underseas navigation, but such a machine has not yet been constructed, although various futile attempts of this kind have been made. With only one system of propulsion we should gain much coveted space and a more evenly distributed weight; within the same dimensions new weapons of attack could be inserted, and also effective weapons of defense. The inventor of such a device would earn a large reward. Let him who wants it, try for it!

Quickly, with deft hands, the outboard connections, which served as exhausts for the oil motors, must be closed in such a way as to resist at once the high water pressure. It is well known that for every ten meters under water we oppose the pressure of one atmosphere — one kilogram to the square centimeter — and we must be prepared to dive to far greater depths.

When all these openings have been carefully closed and fastened, then begins the maneuver of submersion. The sea water is admitted into big open tanks. Powerful suction engines, in the central control of the boat, draw out the air from these tanks so as to increase the rapid inrush of the water. The chief engineer notifies the captain as soon as the tanks are sufficiently filled and an even weight is established so as to steer the boat to the proper depth for attack. Notwithstanding the noise of the machinery, large, wide-open speaking tubes facilitate the delivery of orders between the commander's turret and the Central, and now is the moment the commander gives the order to submerge.

All this may sound very simple and yet there are a great many things to consider. In the same manner in which an airplane is carefully balanced before taking wing into the high regions of the sky, a submarine must be accurately weighed and measured before it descends into the watery depths of the ocean. The briny water of the North Sea weighs far more than the less salty water of the Baltic Sea, whose western basin is composed of practically fresh water. A boat floats higher in the heavily salted waters of the North Sea and lies deeper and plunges farther down in the waters of the Baltic. The same U-boat, therefore, must take into its tanks a greater quantity of water ballast in the North Sea, to be properly weighted, than when diving into fresher waters. Even with small submarines of 400 tons displacement, there is the enormous difference of 10 tons between 1.025 specific weight in the intake of North Sea water and 1.000 specific weight of fresh water. On the other hand, if too much water is admitted into the tanks, the submarine may plunge with great velocity deeper and deeper beyond its appointed depth, and in such a case it might even happen that the hull of the boat could not withstand the overpowering pressure and would be crushed beneath the mass of water. And yet again if too small a quantity of water ballast is admitted into the tanks, the boat may not sink sufficiently below the surface, and thus we could not obtain an invisible attack which is positively necessary for our success.

How much water then must we take in? The answer to this question is a matter of instinct, education, and experience and we must also depend on the cleverly devised apparatus made for this purpose.

The submarine like the airplane must be always maintained at the proper level. The weight of the boat varies continually during a prolonged voyage. Food is devoured and the diving material of the machinery is consumed. The water in which the boat swims continually changes weight and the boat is imperceptibly raised or lowered in a way very difficult to ascertain. The officer responsible for the flooding of the submarine must painstakingly keep its weight under control during the entire navigation. The weight of a meal eaten by each man of the crew, the remains of the food and the boxes in which it was contained, which have been thrown overboard, must be calculated as well as the weight of the water, and the officer employs delicate apparatus for these measurements.

On the open seas these alterations

in weight do not occur very rapidly; but whenever a boat approaches the mouth of a river, then the transition from salt to fresh water happens very suddenly and may provoke the undesirable disturbances to which we have already alluded. Also warm and cold currents at different depths produce thermotic conditions, which surprisingly change the weight of the water.

Peculiar as it may appear, a submarine must be lightened to descend to a very great depth, whereas, in steering to a higher level, more water must be admitted into the tanks to prevent our emerging to the surface with too great suddenness. This demands careful attention, skill, and experience.

The principal condition for the success of a submarine attack is to steer to the exact depth required. The periscope must not rise too far above water, for it might easily be observed by the enemy; but if, by clumsy steering, the top of the periscope descends below the waves, then it becomes impossible to take aim to fire the torpedo. The commander therefore must be able to depend on the two men who control the vertical and horizontal rudders, whom another officer constantly directs and supervises.

When the boat has reached the prescribed depth a close examination is made of all the outward-leading pipes, to see if they can properly resist the water pressure; if any tiny leak has been sprung, every cap must be tightly screwed down; for it is evident it would be very undesirable if any leak should occur and increase the

28

heaviness of the submarine. Absolute silence must prevail so that any dripping or greater influx in the tanks can be observed.

Quietly and silently the boat advances against the enemy; the only audible sounds are the purring of the electric motors and the unavoidable noise made by the manipulation of the vertical and horizontal rudders. Alert and speechless, every man on board awaits a sign from the commander, who is watching in the turret; but some time may elapse — now that the periscope is lowered and nearly on the level of the waters — before the adversary becomes visible again. The ship may have changed her course and have taken an opposite direction to the one she was following at the moment we submerged. In that case she would be out of reach and all our preparations prove useless.

At various intervals, the commander presses an electric button and raises and lowers the periscope as quickly as possible, so as to take his own observation without, if possible, being observed himself; for he knows that any injury to the periscope — his most priceless jewel — would, as it were, render the boat blind and rob him of the much coveted laurel leaves. During these short glimpses the commander only perceives a little sky and the wide, round plate of the reflected sea with its dancing waves, while the nervous tension of the expectant crew increases every minute.

At last is heard a joyous outcry from the commander, "The fellows are coming!" — and after one quick glance, to locate the enemy exactly, the periscope is lowered. Now every heart beats with happy anticipation and every nerve quivers with excitement. The captain quickly issues his orders for the course to be steered and for the necessary navigation. The officer in charge of the torpedoes receives the command to clear the loaded torpedo for firing, while the captain quietly calculates, first, the relative position of his boat to the enemy's ship, according to the course she has taken; secondly, at which point he must aim the torpedo to take surest effect, and — in the same way as in hunting a hare — he withholds the shot to correspond to his victim's gait.

Many thoughts fly through his brain. Here, among his companions, the annihilation of the enemy will cause joyful enthusiasm, while among them their downfall will cause overwhelming sorrow. But without doubt they must vanish from the seas, and only a man, who has experienced these sensations, knows how many secondary matters occur to him at such a time.

With lowered periscope, he sees nothing that goes on above him on the sea, and like a blind man the boat feels its way through the green flood. Every possible event becomes a subject of conjecture. Will the fellow continue on the same course? Has he seen our periscope in the second it was exposed, and is he running away from us? Or, on the contrary, having seen us, will he put on full steam and try to run us down with a fatal death stroke from his prow?

At such an instant of high nervous

tension, I have caught myself giving
superfluous orders to let myself relax,
and yet I knew that every man was at
his post, fully conscious that his own
safety, the safety of the whole boat,
and the honor of the Fatherland were
all at stake, and dependent on his in-
dividual effort. I knew, of course, that
each fine fellow, down in the machinery
room or at the torpedo tubes, had done
his very best, and that all his thoughts
were centered like mine in keen ex-
pectancy on the firing of our first
torpedo — the eel as we call it, guarded
with so much love and care — which
would speed along accompanied by our
warmest wishes. We give nicknames
to our torpedoes, mostly feminine
names: side by side below lie "the
fat Bertha," "the yellow Mary," and
"the shining Emma," and these ladies

expected to be treated, like all ladies, with the tenderest care and courtesy.

Now comes the announcement from the torpedo officer, "The torpedoes are cleared for firing." He stands with a firm hand awaiting the signal from his commander to permit the torpedo to drive ahead against the hated, but unconscious adversary, and to bore its way with a loud report deep into the great steel flank.

Once again the periscope springs for an instant to the surface and then glides back into the protecting body of the turret. The captain exclaims, "We are at them!" and the news spreads like wildfire through the crew. He gives a last rapid order to straighten the course of the boat. The torpedo officer announces, "Torpedo ready"—and the captain, after one quick glance through

34

the periscope, as it slides back into its sheath, immediately shouts, "Fire!"

Even without the prescribed announcement from the torpedo officer that the torpedo had been set off, every one knows that it is speeding ahead, and for a few seconds we remain in anxious suspense, until a dull report provokes throughout our boat loud cheers for Kaiser and for Empire, and by this report we know that "the fat Bertha" has reached unhindered her destination. Radiant with joy, the commander breathes a sigh of relief, and he does not check the young sailor at the wheel, who seeks to grasp his hand and murmur his fervent congratulations. But congratulations must be postponed until we ascertain that our success is complete.

And once again the periscope runs up

towards the laughing daylight, while the commander in happy but earnest tones utters the reassuring words, "The ship is sinking, further torpedoes can be spared." He then permits the gratified torpedo officer, who stands by his side, a quick glance through the periscope to verify the result of his own efficiency. It is chiefly owing to the care of the personnel of the torpedo squad, that the torpedoes are maintained in such perfect condition and that their aim is so correct; and to them is due in great part the success of our attack.

The commander and his officer exchange a knowing look, for they have seen the enemy's ship heavily listing to one side, where the water is rushing into the gaping wound, and soon she must capsize. They see her crew

A TORPEDOED SCHOONER

hastily lowering the life boats — their only means of escape — and this is a sufficient proof of our victory. We can depart now in all security. Concealing our ₁ presence, we plunge and vanish beneath the waters; having reached a certain distance, we stop to make sure that our victim lies at the bottom of the ocean. We behold the waves playing gently and smoothly as before over the cold, watery grave of the once proud ship and we hasten away from the scene of our triumph.

There is no need of our going to the help of the enemy's crew struggling in the sea, for already their own torpedo boats are hurrying to the succor of their comrades, and for us there is further work to be done.

. Imagine the enthusiasm our dear fallen comrade, Weddingen, and his crew must have felt as the loud report of their last torpedo announced the destruction of their third English armed cruiser!

IV

MOBILIZATION AND THE BEGINNING OF THE COMMERCIAL WAR

AFTER long and agitated waiting, we received |in the last days of July, 1914, the command to mobilize. Joyful expectation was visible on every face, and the only fear that prevailed was that those of us who were awaiting our orders on land might be too late to take part in the naval battle we were all looking forward to so eagerly.

A few years ago, one of the Lords of the English Admiralty had predicted that in the first naval battle fought between Germany and England, the German fleet would be entirely anni-hilated. We naturally only smiled in derision at these boastful words. The

English newspapers, besides, had for many years announced that whenever German officers met together they drank a toast "To the Day." Although of course this was untrue, yet we were all burning to prove in battle what our great Navy had learned in long, hard-working years of peace.

A mighty engagement at sea seemed to us imminent during these first days of war, and we all longed to be in it. I was, however, at the moment, among those unfortunates who were strapped down to a desk in the Admiralty, and with envy I beheld my comrades rushing to active service, for I had always hoped to lead my old beloved U-boat victoriously against the enemy. We had all placed strong hopes in the part our submarines would eventually play in a great crisis, but we never

Photograph by Brown & Dawson, Stamford, Conn.
From Underwood & Underwood, N.Y.

GERMAN SUBMARINES U 13, U 5, U 11, U 3, AND U 16 IN KIEL HARBOR

dreamed that they would so successfully take the first rôle as our most
effective weapon in naval warfare.

With a happiness that can hardly
be described, I suddenly received the
order to take over the command of a
fine, new U-boat which had just been
built at Kiel. Never before was a pen
more quickly thrown aside and a desk
closed than when I handed over my
duties in the Admiralty to my suc-
cessor, and shortly afterwards I took
possession of my new, splendid boat,
to which I was going to confide all my
luck and all I was humanly capable
of doing.

I addressed my crew in a short
speech, and told them we could best
serve our Almighty War Lord in bringing this new weapon of attack, confided to our care, to the highest state of

efficiency, and my words were greeted with loud cheers.

There was much work to be done in putting the finishing touches to our submarine, which had only just come off the ways. The auxiliary machines had to be tested and certain inner arrangements made; but, thanks to the untiring zeal of the crew and to the eager help we received from the Imperial Navy Yard, our task was soon accomplished. After a few short trial trips and firing tests, I was able to declare our boat ready for sea and for war, and after everything had been formally surveyed by the inspector we left our home port before the middle of August.

Departing at a high speed, we bade farewell to the big ships still at their moorings, and we soon joined our fellow submarines, who had already in the first fortnight of war, according to an announcement of the Admiralty Staff, made a dash as far as the English coast; and here is the proud record of what they further accomplished: At the beginning of September, 1914, the English cruiser "Pathfinder" was torpedoed by Lieutenant-Captain Hersing, who later sunk the two ships of the line, "Triumph" and "Majestic," in the Dardanelles and was rewarded with our highest order, *Pour le Mérite.*

This initial success proclaimed our submarines to be our greatest weapon of offense and their importance became of world-wide renown, for we claim the honor of having fired the first successful torpedo shot from a submarine. It opened a new era in maritime warfare and was the answer to many questions, which had puzzled the men of our profession the whole world over. Above all, we had proved that a German U-boat, after a long and difficult voyage, could reach the enemy's coast; and after penetrating their line of defense was able to send one of their ships to the bottom of the sea with one well-aimed torpedo shot. The age of the submarine had truly begun.

Other victories followed in prompt succession. Weddingen's wonderful prowess off the Hoek of Holland, on September 22, 1914, will never be forgotten. In the space of an hour he sunk the three English armored cruisers, "Cressy," "Hague," and "Aboukir," and shortly afterwards dispatched their comrade "Hawke" to keep them company at the bottom of the North Sea.

44

Let me add to this list the English cruiser "Hermes" near Dover, the "Niger" off the Downs of the English coast; the Russian cruiser "Pallada" in the Baltic; and a great number of other English torpedo boats, torpedo boat destroyers, as well as auxiliary cruisers and transports. All this was achieved before the end of 1914. Unfortunately I am not at liberty, for obvious reasons, to describe my own part in the beginning of the War, but hope to be able to do so after we achieve a victorious peace.

Our dear cousins on the other side of the Channel must have been rather disquieted by the loss of so much shipping at the hands of our boats or of our mines; and they must have realized that a new method of warfare had begun, for their fleet no longer paraded in the North Sea or in any of the waters in the war zone. Their great, valuable ships were withdrawn, and the patrol of their coast was confided only to smaller craft and to the mine-layers, in order that their people might supposedly sleep in peace.

Our adversary was concealed by day, and only ventured forth at night, confident that darkness would insure his safety. This was then the hour for us to lie in watch for our prey, and no more glorious clarion call could have heralded in the New Year than the torpedo shot, which, on the New Year's Eve of 1915, sent the mighty ship of the line "Formidable" to the bottom of the Channel. This was our first triumphant victory, which showed that not even darkness could circumvent our plans, and which dispelled all

46

further doubts as to our efficiency. A few days after the sinking of the "Formidable" a piece of one of the row boats was washed ashore at Zeebrugge, and now adorns our Sea Museum as the only reminder left of the great ship.

We stood at last on the same footing as our dear old sister, the torpedo boat, to whom we in reality owed our present development, and from now on, in proud independence, we were justified in considering ourselves a separate branch of the Navy.

Now that England felt obliged to withhold the activities of her fleet, she instigated against us the commercial blockade and hunger-war; she obliged neutrals to follow a prescribed route; and, by subjecting their vessels to search, she prevented them from selling us any of their wares.   In this manner,

47

she sought to redeem herself from the paralysis we had brought on her fleet, and her unscrupulous treatment of the right of nations and her interpretation of the so-called "freedom of the seas" are only too well known.

We retaliated on February 4, 1915, by prescribing a certain danger zone, which extended around Great Britain and Ireland and along the north coast of France. By this interdict, public opinion was enlightened as to the part our U-boats were going to perform in this new commercial warfare, a part, I must admit, that few people had anticipated before the commencement of hostilities. Of course, new demands were to be made upon us; we should have to make long undersea trips, and remain for some time in the enemy's waters, after which we should have to return unperceived. The English called it German bluff, but their tone soon changed after we had made our first raid in the heart of the Irish Channel, and few of them now ventured abroad except when forced by the most imperative obligations.

At the end of October, 1914, the first English steamer "Glitra" was sunk off the Norwegian coast. It carried a cargo of sewing machines, whisky, and steel from Leith. The captain was wise enough to stop at the first signal of the commander of the U-boat, and he thereby saved the lives of his crew, who escaped with their belongings after the steamer was peacefully sunk. If others later had likewise followed his example, innocent passengers and crew would not have been drowned; and after all, people are fond of their own lives; but these English captains were following the orders of their Government to save their ships through flight. The English authorities even went so far as to inaugurate a sharp-shooting system at sea by offering a reward to any captain who rammed or destroyed a German submarine, although the latter could only obey this command at the risk of their lives; but what cared the rulers in England for the existence of men belonging to the lower classes of the Nation? They offered tempting rewards for these exploits in the shape of gold watches, and bribed the captains of the merchant marine with the promise of being raised to the rank of officers in the Reserve. Therefore, the British newspapers were filled with the account of the destruction ·of German U-boats, and of the generous rewards given for these fine deeds. It was jolly for us on our return to port to read the record of our own doom, and scarcely would there be a submarine afloat if these records had been true.

I should like to tell a short story in connection with these assertions of English prowess. One of their small steamers had actually contrived in misty weather to ram the turret of one of our submarines while it was in the act of submerging. The English captain was loudly praised in all the newspapers and received the promised rewards for having sunk, as he declared, a German U-boat; he had distinctly felt, he said, the shock of the collision. His statement was certainly accurate, for the submarine was also conscious of the shock, but it was fortunately followed with no evil results, and our commander had the joyful surprise, shortly afterwards, when he emerged, to find the blade of the foe's propeller stuck in the wall of the turret, whose excellent material had preserved it from serious injury. We happily hope that the German Empire will never run so short of bronze that it will be obliged to appropriate, for the melting pot, this fine propeller blade, which is one of the many interesting trophies preserved in our Submarine Museum.

V

OUR OWN PART IN THE COMMERCIAL WAR AND OUR FIRST CAPTURED STEAMER

AS we have said above, our war against the merchant marine of the Allied Nations began in February, 1915, throughout the war zone established around the English and French coasts. Day after day, the number increased of steamers and sail boats that we had sunk, and commercial relations between all countries were seriously menaced. The English were forced to believe in our threats and even the shipping trade of the neutrals had greatly diminished. The mighty British fleet no longer dared to patrol the seas, and the merchantmen were told to look out for themselves and were even armed for the purpose.

While the winter lasted, there was not much for us to do, and we awaited fine weather with lively impatience. During this period, our victorious armies had occupied Belgium and Serbia, and conquered the Russian girdle of fortifications. The subsequent participation of Italy produced but little impression on the fortunate current of events, whereas Turkey's entrance at our side in the war, opened a new field of operation for our U-boats in the Mediterranean.

At last, I, myself, was ordered to prepare for a long voyage, which I welcomed most joyfully after several months of comparative inaction. We were to remain in the enemy's waters for several. weeks, which, of course, involved the most elaborate preparations. Every portion of the boat was again minutely inspected, every machine repaired and thoroughly tested. Like a well-groomed horse we must be in perfect condition for the coming race. Each man in the crew holds a responsible position and knows that the slightest neglect endangers the welfare of the whole boat. The commander must be certain that everything is completed according to the highest standard. The boat is frequently submerged and performs various exercises underseas, while it is still safe in the friendly waters off our own coast.

We are always abundantly provisioned; for the thirty men must be given the most nourishing food to be fit for their arduous tasks. I have often laughed to see the quantity of provisions placed on deck, — for the dealers, of course, are never allowed to penetrate the inner shrine of the boat, — and yet we have often returned from a long cruise because our food was coming to an end. Every available corner and space is filled with provisions. The cook — a sailor specially trained for the job — must hunt below in every conceivable place for his vegetables and meats. The latter are stored in the coolest quarters, next to the munitions. The sausages are put close to the red grenades, the butter lies beneath one of the sailor's bunks, and the salt and spice have been known to stray into the commander's cabin, below his berth.

When everything is in readiness, the crew is given a short leave on land, to go and take the much coveted hot bath. This is the most important ceremony before and after a cruise, especially when the men return, for when they have remained unwashed for weeks, soaked with machine oil, and saturated with salt spray, their first thought is — a hot bath. At sea, we must be very sparing of our fresh-water supply, and its use for washing must be carefully restricted.

The commander usually spends the eve of his departure in the circle of his comrades, but it is a solemn moment for him as soon as he sails from his native shore. He becomes responsible for every action which is taken, and for many weeks no orders reach him from his superiors. He is unable to ask any one's advice, or to consult with his inferiors, and he stands alone in the solitude of his higher rank. Even the common sailor is conscious of the seriousness of the task ahead and of the adventures which may occur below seas. No loud farewells, no jolly hand, no beckoning girls are there to bid us Godspeed. Quietly and silently do we take our departure. Neither wife nor child, nor our nearest and dearest, know whither we go, if we remain in home waters, or if we go forth to encounter the foe. We can bid no one farewell. It is through the absence of news that they know that we have gone, and no one is aware, except the special high officer in this department of the Admiralty who gives the commander his orders, on what errand we are bound or when we shall return, for the slightest indiscretion might forfeit the success of our mission.

Before dawn, on the day of our departure, the last pieces of equipment and of armament are put on board, and the machinery is once more tested; then, at the appointed hour, the chief engineer informs the commander that everything is ready. A shrill whistle bids the crew cast loose the moorings, and at the sound of the signal bell the boat begins to move. As we glide rapidly out of port, we exchange by mutual signs a few last greetings with our less favored comrades on the decks of the ships we leave behind, who no doubt also long to go forth and meet the enemy.

The land begins to disappear in the distance, and as we gaze at the bobbing buoys that vanish in our wake, we hope that after a successful journey they will again be our guides as we return to our dear German homes. After gliding along smoothly at first, we soon feel the boat tossing among the bigger waves; but we laugh, as they heave and dip around us, for we know everything is shipshape on board, and that they can do us no harm. The wild seas are bearing us onward towards the hated foe, and after all — in the end they lull so peacefully to sleep the sailor in his eternal rest.

In this manner, on a fine March morning, we steered our course to the English coast, to take an active part in the commercial war. Gently the waves splashed around the prow and glided over the lower deck. Our duty was to examine every merchantman we met with the object of destroying those of the enemy. The essential thing was to ascertain the nationality of the ships we stopped. On the following morning, we were given several opportunities to fulfill our task.

It is well known that the English merchantmen were ordered by their Government to fly a neutral flag, so as to avoid being captured by our warships. We all remember how, on one of her earlier trips through the war zone, the gigantic "Lusitania" received a wireless message to conceal the Union Jack and to fly the Stars and Stripes of the United States, but destiny after all overtook her at a later date.

All of us U-boat commanders were told not to trust to the nationality of any flag we saw, and to stop every steamer on our path and to examine her papers thoroughly. Even these might be falsified, and we must therefore judge for ourselves, according to the appearance of the crew and the way in which the ship was built, whether she were in reality a neutral. Of course many neutrals had to suffer from the deceptions practiced by the English, and although their colors were painted on their sides and they were lighted at night by electricity, yet this device could also be copied. Therefore, we were obliged to detain and examine all the ships we encountered, greatly to the inconvenience of the innocent ones.

I will describe the manner in which a warship undertakes the search of a merchantman: Through flag signals the merchantman is bidden to stop immediately; if he does not obey, the warship makes his orders more imperative by firing blank shot as a warning. If then the merchantman tries to escape, the warship is justified in hitting the runaway. On the other hand, if the steamer or sailboat obeys the summons, then the warship puts out a boat with an armed prize crew and an officer to look over the ship's papers. These consist in certificates of nationality, of the sailing port, and port of destination, and they contain a bill of lading as to the nature of the cargo, also the names of the crew and a passenger list if it is a passenger steamer. If the ship is a neutral and her papers are satisfactory, she is allowed to proceed, whereas an enemy's ship is either captured or sunk. If a neutral ship carries contraband of war, this is either confiscated or destroyed, but if it exceeds half the total cargo, then this ship is also condemned.

It is nearly impossible for a submarine to send a prize crew on board a big ship, therefore neutral States have given their captains the order to go in a ship's boat and deliver their papers themselves on board the submarine; but they often annoyed us by a long parley and delay, and it was always with a feeling of disappointment that we were obliged to leave inactive our cannons and torpedoes, the crew sadly exclaiming, "After all, they were only neutrals!"

One sunny afternoon, we were in the act of examining the papers of a Dutch steamer that we had stopped in the neighborhood of the Meuse Lightship, when we perceived on the horizon another steamer coming rapidly towards us, and we judged by its outline that it was of English construction. The steamer we were examining proved to be unobjectionable in every respect, and sailing only between neutral ports, so we dismissed it, and just as it was departing, the English steamer, evidently apprehending our presence, turned about in great haste in hope to escape from us, and steered with full steam ahead towards the English shores, to seek the protection of the ships on the watch patroling the English coast.

The English captain well knew what fate awaited him if he fell into the hands of a wicked German U-boat. Mighty clouds of smoke rose from her funnels, giving evidence of the active endeavors of the stokers in the boiler-room to bring the engines up to their highest speed, and before we had time to give the signal to stop, the steamer was in flight.

Meanwhile we had also put on all steam in pursuit, and drove our engines to their utmost capacity. The English

65

ship was going at a great pace, and we had many knots to cover before we could catch up with her to impose our commands, for she paid no heed to the international flag-signal we had hoisted —"Stop at once or we fire!"— and she was striving her uttermost to reach a zone of safety. Our prow plunged into the surging seas, and showered boat and crew alike with silvery, sparkling foam. The engines were being urged to their greatest power, and the whir of the propeller proved that below, at the motor valves, each man was doing his very best. Anxiously, we measured the distance that still separated us from our prey. Was it diminishing? Or would they get away from us before our guns could take effect? Joyfully we saw the interval lessening between us, and before long our first warning shot, across her bow, raised a high, threatening column of water. But still the Englishman hoped to escape from us, and the thick smoke belching from the funnels showed that the stokers were shoveling more and more coal into the glowing furnace; they well knew what risk they had to run.

Even after two well-aimed shots were discharged from the steel mouths of our cannons, right and left on either side of the fugitive, which must have warned the captain that the next shot would undoubtedly strike the stern, he was still resolved neither to stop nor surrender.

Nothing now remained for us but to use our last means to enforce our will. With a whistling sound, a shell flew from the muzzle of our cannon and a few seconds later fell with a loud crash in a cloud of smoke on the rear deck of the steamer. This produced the desired effect.

Immediately the steamer stopped and informed us by three quick blasts from the steam whistle (the international signal) that the engines would be reversed and the ship stopped. The captain had given up his wild race.

Huge white clouds from the uselessly accumulated steam rose from the funnels, and to our signal, "Abandon the ship at once," the Englishman replied with a heavy heart by hoisting a white and red striped pennon, the preconcerted international sign that our order had been understood and was being obeyed.

This small striped pennon has a deep significance: it means that a captain accepts this most painful necessity knowing that his dear old boat will soon lie at the bottom of the sea; truly a difficult decision for the captain of a proud ship to make. The crew were by this time reconciled to their fate and, as we drew near to parley with the captain, the life boats were launched; the men tossed in their belongings and, jumping in, took their places at the oars. It need hardly be said that we, on the other hand, were pleased with our capture. I have often shaken hands with the gunner who had fired the last deadly shot, for we waste no emotion over our adversary's fate. With every enemy's ship sent to the bottom, one hope of the hated foe is annihilated. We simply pay off our account against their criminal wish to starve all our people, our women, and our children, as they are unable to beat us in open fight with polished steel. Ought we not therefore to rejoice in our justifiable satisfaction?

After the crew had left in two boats the blazing hull of the "Leuwarden" of Harwich, a well-directed shot was aimed at the water line. Mighty jets of water poured into the rear store-room, and the heavy listing of the ship showed that her last hour had struck. We beckoned to the captain to row up beside us and deliver his papers; he stepped silently on board, and we exchanged salutes. As I saw that the two boat-loads of twenty-five men were lying off within hearing, on either side of us, I took this opportunity to admonish the captain about his foolhardy attempt to escape, and how he thereby had endangered the lives of his crew. The latter, realizing the justice of my remarks, thanked us for having saved them by respectfully lifting their caps. The captain awkwardly excused himself by saying he had simply hoped to get away.

I then notified these people whom we had saved that we would take them in tow to the Meuse Lightship; at this, the fine-looking old captain realized to what useless dangers he had exposed his men, and what cause he had to be grateful to us. With tears in his eyes. he seized my hand and murmured his thanks. I willingly took his outstretched hand. . . . At that instant a Dutch pilot steamboat, which had been attracted to the spot by the sound of firing, hove in sight, and I committed the Englishmen to its care. We all desired, before departing in opposite directions, to witness the final sinking of the steamer, for apparently the English also wanted to see the last of their fine ship, and we awaited the great moment in silence.

We had not long to wait. The stern of the ship sank deeper and deeper, whereas the bow rose sharply in the air, till at last with a loud gurgle the whole steamer was drawn down, and the waters bubbled and roared over the sunken wreck. There was now one less fine ship of the English merchant marine afloat on the ocean!

We had all seen enough, and each one went his way. Our course was pointed westward towards new endeavors, while the Dutchman steered for the nearest port in order to land the shipwrecked crew. I think it was our English friends who waved a friendly farewell from the deck of the pilot steamboat in grateful recognition for our having saved their lives, although they may not actually have wished us "*aufwiedersehn.*"

We read in the Dutch papers a few days later an accurate description of the sinking of the "Leuwarden," and the English captain was fain to acknowledge how well we had treated him; every captain of an English steamer might have been treated in like manner had not the English Government wished it otherwise.

VI

THE CAPTURE OF TWO PRIZE STEAMERS

THE next day an opportunity offered itself to us which opened to submarines a new field of activity in the commercial war. It was a gray, misty morning, the sea was becalmed, and over the still waters a heavy vapor hung low like a veil before the rising sun. But little could be seen, and we had to keep a sharper lookout than usual to avoid running unawares into a hostile ship, and we also had to be ready for a sudden submersion. We strained all the more an attentive ear to every sound; for it is well known that in a fog, during a calm, we sailors can perceive the most distant noise that comes over the water. In time of peace fog horns and whistles give warning of any approaching vessel, but in time of war, on the contrary, no vessel wishes to betray its presence. It is essential for us to have two men down below, at listening posts, with their ears glued to the sides of the boat, to catch the throbbing of a propeller, or the rush of waves dashing against the prow of a ship, or any suspicious vibrations, for these noises are easily discernible under sea, water being an excellent sound conductor.

On this March morning we were all keenly intent on the approach of some ship; many times already as we stood on the bridge we had been deceived by some unreal vision or some delusive sound; our overstrained nerves transformed our too lively fancy into seeming reality; and in a thick fog objects are strangely magnified and distorted: a floating board may assume the shape of a boat, or a motor launch be taken for a steamer.

I remember a little story about a man-of-war seeking to enter a harbor in a heavy fog; every one on board was looking in vain for a buoy to indicate the channel when the captain himself called out, "It is for me then to point out the buoy; there it is!" but as they drew near, the buoy floating on the water spread out a pair of wings and flew away in the shape of a gull; and many a gull in a fog may have deceived other experienced seamen.

But to return to our own adventures on this misty morning; we not only saw gulls rising from the sea, and boards floating on the water, but we also encountered English mines adrift, which had parted from their moorings, and to these we thought it safer to give a wide berth. At last the fog lifted, and we discovered in the distance, a few knots away, a steamer; we immediately went in pursuit. Rapidly it steamed ahead, but we caught up with it, and found it belonged to the Dutch-Batavian Line, but as it was steering for the English coast, towards the mouth of the Thames, we took for granted it carried a contraband cargo. We signaled for it to stop, but the steamer refused to obey our command and increased its speed. Having ascertained that we could easily overtake it, we spared our shot, which must be carefully preserved for more useful purposes. After a chase which lasted about three quarters of an hour only a thousand meters remained between us. The Dutch captain wisely gave up a further attempt to escape, and awaited our orders. In compliance with my signal he sent his first officer in a boat with the ship's papers. While we lay alongside the steamer, gently rocking to and fro, the crew and passengers flocked on deck to gaze at us with wondering eyes, and we in return tried to discover to what nationality they belonged.

On reading the papers the officer handed me, I saw the steamer was the "Batavian IV," destined for London, carrying a cargo of provisions, which is contraband of war. I had to make a rapid decision as to the fate of the steamer, and I resolved to bring the "Batavian" into one of the Belgian ports now in our possession. No

THE START: TAKING IN OIL FROM HER TENDER

THE CHASE: FOLLOWING IN THE WAKE OF A DUTCH STEAMER

OVERHAULING HER PREY: ROUNDING THE BOW OF THE
BATAVIER IV

THE SUMMONS TO SURRENDER: CALLING UPON THE STEAMER
TO HEAVE TO

VON FORSTNER'S SUBMARINE (U 28)

A Series of Photographs taken from

PREY NUMBER TWO: APPROACHING THE ZAANSTROOM

ABOUT TO BOARD THE PRIZE: THE PILOT LEAVING THE
TENDER FOR THE STEAMER

THE TRIUMPH: THE SUBMARINE LEADING THE WAY THROUGH
MINE-FIELDS INTO ZEEBRÜGGE

IN ACTION IN THE NORTH SEA

the Deck of One of her Victims

U-boat had ever attempted such a feat before, but why not try? Of course we had to cover a long distance with the imminent threat of being overtaken by English warships, but if we did succeed, it was a very fine catch, and after all, — nothing venture, nothing have. Besides the misty weather was in our favor, and it would only take a few hours to reach the protection of our batteries on the Flemish coast.

The Dutch officer was notified that a prize crew would be at once sent on board his steamer to conduct it to the port of Zeebrugge. He opened wondering eyes, but made no protest, for he was fully aware of our cannons turned on his ship and of the loaded pistols of our crew. The crew and passengers on board the Dutchman were no less astounded when our prize command, consisting of one officer and one sailor, climbed up on deck. I could not well dispense, myself, with more men, and in case my prize was released by the English, it would be better they had so few prisoners of ours to take.

The Dutch captain raised several objections at being led away captive in this manner; above all he was afraid of the German mines strewn before the entrance of Zeebrugge, but my officer reassured him by telling him we should lead the way and he would therefore run no risk. He finally had to resign himself to his fate. So we proceeded towards the shores of Flanders; we, in the proud consciousness of a new achievement, and the Dutchman lamenting over the seizure of his valuable cargo. The passengers must have wondered what was in store for them. Many of the ladies were lightly clad, having been roused in fright from their morning slumbers, and their anxious eyes stared at us, while we merrily looked back at them.

Our officer on board exchanged continual signals with us, and we were soon conscious, with a feeling of envy, as we gazed through our field glasses, that he was getting on very friendly terms with the fair sex on board our prize. We had feared at first that he might have some disagreeable experiences, but his first message spelled, "There are a great many ladies on board," and the second, "We are having a delicious breakfast," and the third, "The captain speaks excellent German," so after this we were quite reassured concerning him.

An hour may have elapsed when a cloud of smoke on the eastern horizon announced the approach of another steamer, and the idea that we might perhaps capture a second prize ship was very alluring. The wisdom of abandoning for a while our first captive was considered somewhat doubtful; if we delayed it might escape after darkness set in, but when I heard my officers exclaim "What a fine steamer!" I decided to try for it. The "Batavian" was ordered to proceed slowly on the same course, and we would catch up with it later; then turning my attention to steamer No. 2, I made quickly in her direction to intercept her on her way to England. After half an hour's pursuit we signaled for her to stop, and we discovered she was also Dutch. The captain, seeing it was useless to try and escape, put out a boat and came on board with the ship's papers; he seemed thoroughly displeased at the meeting, and hoped no doubt by coming himself to get away more easily, but of this expectation he was to be sadly disabused. On discovering that he was also carrying contraband of war — cases of eggs for London — I ordered him to follow us to Zeebrugge. One officer and a stoker, for I could not spare another sailor, accompanied him as our prize command on board his ship, the "Zaanstroom," and after a lapse of an hour and a half, followed by No. 2, we caught up with No. 1.

The difficulty of my task can be easily imagined, for I was obliged to make the two steamers follow each other at a given interval and at the same speed; like a shepherd dog herding his flock I had to cruise round my two captives and force them to steer a straight and even course, for one tried occasionally to outdistance the other, probably with the desire to escape in the foggy weather, which increased my fear of not reaching the Flemish coast before dark.

But finally I got the steamers into line, and where persuasion might have failed the menace of my cannons was doubtless my surest reason for success.

My second officer on the "Zaanstroom" signaled that everything was going to his liking and that they were just sitting down to a savory meal of dropped eggs. This was reassuring news, and I could also feel tranquil on his behalf; besides in a few hours we should be safely under cover of our coast artillery. We notified the Pilot Depot by wireless to send us a pilot for each ship, and our messages having been acknowledged we were certain of being warmly welcomed, and that every preparation would be made for the reception of our two prizes.

The closer we got to the coast the heavier the fog lay upon the water, a not unusual experience at sea. We had to advance with the greatest caution; our U-boat led the way to confirm anew the assurance we had given our two steamers that they were in no danger of mines. We had to measure the depth of water repeatedly with the lead, and so doing we had to stop very often; otherwise the lead being dragged by the current draws the line to an inaccurate length. It is but too easy a matter to run aground off the coast

85

of Flanders, as submerged sandbanks are everywhere to be encountered, and this would have been in our present case a most unfortunate occurrence. This continual stopping rather disturbed the order of our march, for steamers are more unwieldy and less accustomed to rapid maneuvering than war vessels. Luckily all went well with us, for after a fine trip of several hours we gladly greeted our German guardships lying off the port of Zeebrugge, and the lighthouse on the mole beckoned to us from afar through the thin afternoon mist.

We quickly surrendered our two captives to the patrol of the port authorities, into whose care and surveillance they were now entrusted. Our job for the day was over, and we could joyfully hurry to our berth within the harbor. We passed along the tremendous stone quay of the artificial port of Zeebrugge; it extends several kilometers, and was built by Leopold II with English money; it had cost many, many millions, and was intended to serve quite another purpose than its present one. We could look with defiance at the mouth of our German cannons that gaped over the highest edge of the jetty towards the sea, as if awaiting the foe.

Farther on up the mole, instead of English troops that the King would so gladly have sent over in transports to march through neutral Belgium and pay us an uninvited visit, stood, side by side, our own brave fellows of the Army and of the Navy. Men from every branch of the service, in their different uniforms, were visible, as they crowded on the pier to witness our arrival with our two prize boats, for the news of this unusual capture had already spread far and wide, and they all wanted to satisfy their curiosity. Their enthusiasm would have been even greater had they guessed that concealed within the hull of our two vessels an Easter feast of undreamed-of dainties lay in store for them. But even without this incentive a tremendous cheer from a thousand throats hailed our appearance as we rounded the mole, and our thirty voices returned as hearty, if not as loud, a three times repeated cheer for the garrison of Zeebrugge. Our tow lines were caught by the eager hands of the sailors, and in a jiffy we were lying securely alongside the quay, safe in port to rest in peace a day or two after a many days' cruise enlivened by such exciting events. Our friends of the Navy, whom we had not seen since the beginning of the war, came to visit us at once; much gay news was exchanged and also sad regrets expressed at the loss of dear fallen comrades.

Shortly afterwards one of the Dutch captains, escorted by two guards, asked me to grant him an interview, and I was glad to make his personal acquaintance; we discussed over a little glass of port wine, which we were both surely entitled to, the incidents of the day, and he gave vent to his affliction at being thus seized, by ejaculating: "A great steamer like mine to be captured by a little beast like yours!" I could sympathize with his feelings, for he had sustained a severe pecuniary loss, and he well knew what would become of his ship and cargo according to prize law, but I suspected he found some consolation in having a companion in misfortune, for the other Dutch captain had to submit to the same conditions. We shook hands and parted excellent friends, knowing that each one of us had only accomplished his duty.

Before making my official report I inspected my two prizes that were docked just behind us; a chain parted them from the rest of the quay, with sentries placed on guard. I gave the preference of my first visit, naturally, as a polite man should, to the steamer with so many of the fair sex on board. I hoped that by appearing surrounded by my officers I should dispel their fear of the "German barbarians." I was told the ladies belonged to a variety troupe that was to give a performance the next evening in London. Poor London, to be deprived by our fault of an enjoyable evening!

Among the other passengers were Belgians and French, who had waited six weeks in Holland for a chance to get across, and also an American reporter of the Hearst newspaper. He had a camera for taking moving pictures, and we discovered later that he had photographed the whole occurrence of the capture of the ship by our submarine. A few days later the *Graphic* of March 27, 1915, published several of his pictures, which eventually found their way to many American papers.

I was ordered that evening to dine with the Commanding Admiral of the Marine Corps, Excellency von Schröder, and a motor called for me and took me to Brügge where he resided. The peaceful landscape and the ploughed fields betrayed but few signs of war, and I saw Belgian peasants and German soldiers planting together the seed for the coming harvest.

While the authorities were passing judgment on my two prizes I had a chance to visit the surrounding country. The English had destroyed in their retreat everything in Zeebrugge, except the new Palace Hotel, the new Post Office, and the Belgian Bank. I made the most of this short opportunity to observe the doings of our men in this conquered land paid for with German blood. I was interested to note how our Marines had been incorporated in every branch of the Army service, and how easily they adapted themselves to this new life. They served as infantry in the trenches, as artillery behind the great coast guns, and also as cavalry mounted on big Flemish mares. They had even been transformed into car conductors on the electric line that runs behind the dunes between Zeebrugge and Ostend. In fact they filled every kind of position, and few Belgians were to be seen. We had created here a second German fatherland and home, notwithstanding the enemy's reports that we had acted like Huns and barbarians, but as neither the country nor the people were of great interest to me my attention was centered on the study of our own troops.

Meantime the unloading of our steamers had begun and I had to supervise it myself. As the cargoes were composed of perishable foodstuffs the usual delays were overcome, and hundreds of sailors and soldiers were ordered to unload the ships. Out of the hold rose newly slaughtered pigs, and sheep, and ducks, which were at once distributed among the various regiments. Two hundred barrels of the best Munich beer were rolled over the quays, and two barrels found their way on board our little boat, which no one could begrudge us. On the "Zaanstroom" there were 4,400 boxes of fresh eggs, each box containing 1,800 eggs, and I was told by an Army officer that every man of the Northern Army received eight eggs for the Easter festival.

On the following afternoon the nationality of the crew and of the passengers was recorded; a number of them were sent as prisoners of war to concentration camps, and many touching farewells ensued between the men and the women who were left behind. The others were taken on a special train under military guard to the Dutch frontier. The German sailors on whom this mission devolved looked very jolly as they sat armed to the teeth in the railway carriages, by twos, watching over two pretty variety actresses, and I think they would willingly have prolonged the journey farther.

I walked along the train to say goodbye to the passengers, who had so unwillingly made our acquaintance, and I was warmly thanked by an old American, to whom I personally had done a small favor, for my courteous treatment; he spoke in the name of all the passengers who had experienced also the greatest civility at the hands of the port authorities. I declined these words of thanks, for they had only received the treatment that was their proper due.

After the train had left, the hour of our own departure had struck; we cast off the lines that had kept us bound for two such memorable days on the Flemish coast. In passing by, I waved a farewell to the two Dutch captains, and away we went — westward ho!

VII

OFF THE COAST OF ENGLAND

OUR boat carried us speedily away farther and farther towards the west, and soon the lighthouse on the mole and the outline of the country we had conquered faded away in the evening twilight. Before long we should be surrounded by only hostile shores.

We first sighted the French port of Boulogne where the imposing bronze statue of Napoleon I stands on a marble column fifty-three meters high, with eyes turned towards the English coast. It was built to commemorate the expedition planned by Napoleon in 1803 against the sons of Albion, whose descendants have so recently landed on

97

French soil, and as they lie there encamped, they may wonder, when gazing at the statue of the great Emperor, if he would have welcomed them with the same enthusiasm with which they have been received by the present rulers of France.

On our very first day in the French Channel we were able to sink several steamers, after the crews had left in their lifeboats, and on general lines a similar picture was traced at every sinking. We were now granted our first opportunity to steer a submarine above and below the waters of the North Atlantic. The ocean seemed to rejoice at our coming, and revealed itself to us in all the glory of a March storm. Only those who have seen such a storm can realize its proud majesty. The gigantic, blue-black waves, with

LIFEBOAT LEAVING THE SINKING P. AND O. LINER ARABIA

their shining crests lashed by the west wind, came rushing onwards into the open mouth of the Channel, and the hemmed-in waters, roaring and surging, dashed themselves against the sharp, rocky points of the French coast, or broke less violently but in ceaseless unrest on the chalk cliffs of England which glimmered white in the rays of the sun.

It is a splendid sight to watch this great spectacle from the high deck of a steamer as it ploughs its way through the foaming flood, or to be borne aloft on the top of the waves with a ship under full sail, but it is still more wonderful to behold Nature's great display from the half submerged conning-tower of a U-boat, and to dive through the mountainous breakers until they close gurgling over our heads and hide us from all curious glances. Our little nutshell, in perpetual motion, is drawn down into the deep valleys of the ocean waves, or tossed upwards on the comb of the following breaker. We are soaked to the skin, and the spray covers us like a silvery veil; our boat as well as ourselves is daubed with a salt crust, our eyes smart and our lips have a briny tang, but to us sailors it's a joy to be the sport of the wild waves, and even those few unfortunates who always suffer from sea-sickness never lose their love of the sea.

We were thus, in the midst of a strong southwesterly gale, lying in wait for our prey at the entrance of the English Channel, but no ship was to be seen; most of them took the northerly course beyond the war zone, around the Shetland Islands, and it was not until the next morning, north of the Scilly Isles, in the Bristol Channel, that we caught sight behind us of a big steamer, running before the wind, like ourselves. The wind had somewhat fallen and the March sun was shining bright and warm; the steamer was heading for Cardiff, and we judged by her course that she had sailed from some port in South America.

Turning about and breasting the waves we faced the oncoming steamer and signaled to her to stop; but hardly had she espied us than she also turned about in the hope to escape. She showed no flag to indicate her nationality, so surely we had sighted an English vessel. Even after we had fired a warning shot, she tried by rapid and tortuous curves to return to her former course, and endeavor thereby to reach her home port. Meantime she sent up rockets as signals of distress in quick succession, to draw the attention of British patrol ships that must be hovering in the neighborhood.

This obliged us to fire a decisive shot, and with a loud report our first shell struck the ship close to the captain's bridge. Instead of resigning himself to his fate, the Englishman sent up more signals and hoisted the British flag. This showed us he was game, and the fight began in dead earnest. All honor to the pluck of these English captains! —but how reckless to expose in this manner the lives of their passengers and crew, as we shall see in the present instance.

Circling around us he tried to ram us with his prow, and we naturally avoided him by also turning in the same direction. Every time he veered about he offered us his broadside for a shot; with well-directed aim we took advantage of this target, and our successful fire gave him full proof of the skill of our gunners. The latter had a hard time of it; the high seas poured over the low deck, and they continually stood up to their necks in the cold salt water. They were often dragged off the deck by the great receding waves, but as they were tied by strong ropes to the cannons we were able to pull them up again, and fortunately no lives were lost.

On seeing our gunners struggling in the seas, our foe hoped to make good his escape, but with each telling shot our own fighting blood was aroused and the wild chase continued. A well-aimed shell tore off the English flagstaff at the stern, but the Union Jack was quickly hoisted again on the foretop. This was also shot down, and a third time the flag flew from a line of the yard of the foretop, but the flag had been raised too hastily and it hung reversed, with the Union Jack upside down, and in this manner it continued to fly until it sank with the brave ship.

The fight had lasted four hours without our being able to deliver the death stroke. Several fires had started on the steamer, but the crew had been able to keep them under control; big holes gaped open in the ship's side, but there were none as yet below the water line, and the pumps still sufficed to expel the water. It often occurred that in the act of firing the waves choked our cannons, and the shot went hissing through tremendous sheets of water, while we were blinded by a deluge of foam. Of course we were all wet, through and through, but that was of no importance, for we had already been wet for days.

It was now essential for us to put an end to this deadly combat, for English torpedo-boat destroyers were hurrying on to the calls of distress of the steamer. Big clouds of smoke against the sky showed they were coming towards us under full steam. The ship was by this time listing so heavily that it was evident we need waste no more of our ammunition, and besides the appearance of another big steamer on the southern horizon was an enticing inducement to quit the battle scene and seek another victim. We cast a last look on our courageous adversary who was gradually sinking, and I must add it was the first and last prey whose end we did not have the satisfaction to witness. We had been truly impressed by the captain's brave endurance, notwithstanding his lack of wisdom, and we knew that the men-of-war were coming to his rescue. We read in the papers, on our return to a German port, that the "Vosges" had sunk soon after we had departed, and what remained of the passengers and crew were picked up by the English ships. The captain was rewarded for his temerity by being raised to the rank of Reserve officer, and the crew were given sums of money; but all the other officers had perished, as well as several sailors and a few passengers, who had been forced to help the stokers in order to increase the speed of the flying steamer.

We hurried away, therefore, in the direction of the other ship, and as we approached we soon recognized the Spanish colors flying from her flagstaff and painted on her sides. The captain willingly stopped at our bidding and dispatched an officer to us bearing the ship's papers. The stormy waves had somewhat subsided, and although the occupants of the boat got very wet, yet they were able, without danger, to come alongside our submarine. There was no contraband on board the Spanish steamer, and before dismissing the officer I admonished him always to stop at the first signal from a U-boat; he assured me that since the English were constantly hoisting the Spanish flag he had lost all desire to navigate again in the dangerous waters of the war zone. Much relieved at getting away so easily he went on board his own steamer, which resumed its voyage towards the lovely city of Santander on the Spanish coast.

I read an account later of our encounter with the "Agustina" in a number of the *Matin* of April 1, 1915. It was entitled *"Toujours l'U"* and spoke of our undesirable presence in French waters; a following number did us the honor to represent a large picture of our boat with the officers standing on the bridge, taken probably by a passenger on board the Spanish vessel. An arrow pointed to us with the inscription, *" Voila l'équipage de bandits."* The English usually refer to us as "the pirates," and in their rage describe our activities as those of the "German submarine pest." We are accustomed to these flattering allusions, and it amused me to preserve and frame our picture from the *Matin*.

In the next few days we stopped and searched several neutral steamers, and sank many English ones. The captains were occasionally stubborn and refused to obey our signals, so a few accidents occurred; in one case, for instance, a stray shot struck some passengers in a lifeboat, which collapsed; but as a rule passengers and crews were picked up by the many sailboats and fishing boats which circulate in the Irish Sea and in St. George's Channel, and it was we who generally summoned these fishermen to go to the rescue of their shipwrecked countrymen.

The method of capture was always the same, and now, our ammunition being nearly exhausted, we steered a homeward course, with the hope of securing a few more steamers on the way. We were again favored by good luck, for at the entrance of the English Channel we ran across a large steamer, coming from America and heading for a French port, heavily laden with all the fine things that the Americans at present so willingly export.

The chase began in the usual fashion as we followed closely in the enemy's wake. Although the captain made an effort to escape, yet he evidently felt certain from the beginning that he would be unable to do so, for he immediately swung out the lifeboats, ready to be lowered. We were economizing our ammunition and did not, according to our custom, fire a warning shot, but as we drew near the steamer we suddenly saw dark, round objects thrown overboard. The man at the helm beside me exclaimed: "They are throwing mines," but I was not of the same opinion. We proceeded quietly to examine these suspicious objects more closely, and we discovered they were simply bundles of clothes the sailors were trying to save. In pitching them into the lifeboats they had missed the mark and the bundles had fallen into the sea. A report had apparently spread through the English seaports that the men had but scant time to save their belongings when they were sighted by one of our submarines, and since that time their clothes were strapped together ready for a sudden emergency. The steamer stopped and the crew on this occasion took to the boats with a perfect discipline we were little accustomed to witness; the "Flaminian" was sent to the bottom of the sea with one of our last torpedoes.

The following morning, before bidding the west coast of England a temporary farewell, we made another good catch. We sighted a broad-bottomed, four-masted steamer, also coming from America, laden down, as we soon ascertained, with 5,000 tons of oats, and making its way to Havre. We started after it, and as usual it tried to escape, but a well-directed shot through the bridge and chart house brought it to a stop, and it signaled that the engines were being reversed. The boats were lowered, and on drawing near we perceived the captain with others on the bridge holding up their hands as a token of surrender. As soon as those on board had taken their places in the lifeboats they rowed

towards us and showed the liveliest
interest in the final torpedoing of their
steamer. They looked upon it as a
new kind of sport, and under the
present conditions they could watch
the performance in the most comfort-
able way. The sea was like a mirror,
and reflected the smiling spring sunshine whose warming rays were most
agreeably felt.

The English captain had scarcely
been on board my submarine a moment
when he begged that we might go
together and verify the excellent aim
of our first shot through the forward
part of his ship, which he told me had
nearly grazed his ear. I consented to
go on his lifeboat and admire with him,
to our mutual enjoyment, the irre-
proachable marksmanship of my gunner, although I did not accept a drink

of whisky one of the English officers offered me.

On seeing the gaping hole in the forecastle, the captain and his men clapped their hands and cried out, "A very good shot!" The captain congratulated me for securing, as he asserted, the richest prize I had ever made, but I assured him we had sunk even more valuable cargoes than the present one. I decided, as the sea was calm and no ship was in sight, to spare our torpedoes and shells and to put an end to the steamer with little hand grenades. The Englishmen took a sportsmanlike interest in the proceedings, and one of the officers even volunteered to show me the most effective position for the explosive. I naturally did not gratify his wish to place it there himself, for I knew myself

very accurately the most vulnerable
spot in the ship.   In a very few moments a big hole was torn in the side
of the "Crown of Castille" and with
a gurgling sound the waters rushed in.
At the same time long, yellow threads
of the finest oats floated far out on
the sea and, glistening with a golden
shimmer, gave proof long after the
steamer had sunk of the precious cargo
which had lain within its flanks.   You
poor French army horses, I fear your
rations were cut short for a while!

I had made an interesting study of
the manner in which the English crews
of the present day were composed.
Apart from the British officers there
were but few experienced seamen on
board.   This was made evident by the
awkward way the men usually handled
the lifeboats.   Even with the enormous

increase of wages, sailors could not be found to risk their lives in the danger zone, and a lot of untrained fellows, negroes and Chinamen, revealed by their clumsy rowing that they had only recently been pressed into service.

Various other interesting incidents occurred on our return trip, which I shall not mention now, but having safely reached our newly conquered port of Ostend, we read to our amusement in a French paper that our U-boat had been sunk in the Channel by a fleet of six fishing steamers.

We were again warmly welcomed by our comrades from the Army and Navy, all anxious to hear the news we had to tell, and we had the special honor of a visit from H.R.H. the Crown Prince Rupprecht of Bavaria, who, after inspecting our boat, permitted me to give him a detailed account of our recent splendid cruise.

We had many other experiences during the quiet, warm, summer months, with their long, clear nights, which enabled us to achieve the further destruction of a large number of steamers. It was glorious to work in fine weather on our U-boat on the waters of the Atlantic Ocean, so peaceful at this season of the year, and so doing we indulged in much friendly intercourse with the various fishermen we met.

Fishing steamers have replaced the old sailboats to a great extent, and they represent an enormous fishing industry. Our larder was daily replenished with fresh fish, which was a greatly appreciated item on our monotonous bill of fare.

One windy evening in August, we

captured a Belgian steamer bringing home coal from Cardiff; the crew having left the ship, the latter was rapidly sinking, when to our astonishment a man sprang on deck from below. He had evidently been forgotten and our shot going through the steamer had warned him of his danger. He hesitated to obey my repeated orders to jump overboard, until finally encased in two life belts he plunged into the water and began to swim; but the screw was still slowly revolving, and he was drawn deep down by the suction of the water. We had given him up as lost, when we were amazed to see him reappear on the other side of the ship. The screw, which had slowly pulled him down, had thrown him up again, and he swam towards us. A big wave having tossed him onto our low deck, we were glad to find he was unhurt, and we gave him the best of care. He was a Dutchman, and after a fortnight spent in our midst, he was so happy he no longer wished to leave us.

When it came to our sinking of the "Midland Queen" a similar incident occurred. A negro had been forgotten by his white fellow-countrymen, and on finding himself abandoned and alone he was so greatly scared that he did not dare to leave the sinking ship; we watched him, and beckoned to him to come to us; but he refused, and swore at us furiously. Presently the "Midland Queen" pitched violently forward, and stood nearly erect with her nose in the water; then with a shrill whistling sound she dived below the surface of the waves. The negro's black head vanished in the turmoil of the waters;

then suddenly a loud detonation occurred; an explosion of compressed air within the ship threw up, sky-high, barrels and boards, and among them, to our unbelieving eyes, we saw the wriggling body of the negro. He was projected into the sea, and swam towards us, apparently none the worse after this strange and violent experience. We rescued him and handed him over to his mates, who had rowed back to his assistance.

On our return voyage through the North Sea we met a large sailboat, with the Swedish flag flying from the topmast. She lay completely becalmed, and signaled for us to draw near. We saw a large crowd gathered on her deck, and we approached cautiously, fearing some trap; when to our joyful surprise we found she had 150 German officers and sailors on board. They belonged to one of our auxiliary cruisers, the "Meteor." Her captain after many exploits had been pursued by several English cruisers, and to save his little vessel from being captured he had deliberately sent her to the bottom of the sea, and the Swedish sailboat had picked up the crew. Our shipwrecked comrades told us they were desperately hungry, but our own provisions were exhausted; so we took them in tow, for not a breath of wind stirred the sails.

By clear sunshine we merrily covered the short distance to our nearest port, and towards midday the sailing ship and ourselves let down our anchors once more off the German coast.

VIII

THE METHOD OF SINKING AND RAISING SHIPS

DURING the present naval warfare we have had the opportunity to watch the sinking of ships of every type and size; shortly after receiving their death wound the vessels usually disappear totally beneath the surface. It takes even big steamers only between four and ten minutes to sink, after being hit by a torpedo or shell beneath the water line, and yet occasionally a ship may float several hours before going down to the bottom of the sea.

It is clearly evident that the slow or rapid sinking of a ship depends on the distribution of its bulkheads and water-tight compartments. A man-of-war, built on the latest models, has a great many small water-tight compartments, for she is meant to be able to continue fighting even after several of these compartments have been destroyed; whereas, an ocean steamer is so constructed that she will remain afloat only a short time after a collision with another ship, or if she runs into an iceberg or a derelict, she can endure a certain intake of water, and lists at a moderate angle far more readily than a warship, whose guns are rendered nearly useless if the ship is heavily canting. A warship must be built so as to withstand, without sinking, the injury caused by a number of gun holes even beneath the water line, where the inner part of the ship must necessarily be subdivided into many parts. A warship is built at great cost, but so is an ocean steamer. The sunken "Lusitania" was worth 35,000,-000 marks (nearly $9,000,000) and the mammoth steamers of the Hamburg-American Line, the "Imperator," the "Vaterland," were still more expensive to build.

The ordinary commercial steamer often has in her inner construction only athwartship bulkheads through the double bottom that run from one side to another and form large partitions; and in proportion to her height a steamer is again subdivided horizontally into several decks. But these are not usually water-tight, and the cross bulkheads already mentioned form the only water-tight divisions in the hold. In the big cargo spaces, these divisions practically do not exist, and the ship, throughout almost its whole interior, is open from keel to deck. This arrangement, of course, facilitates the rapid loading and unloading of the cargo; therefore, in this type of ship the engine rooms and boilers, surrounded and protected by coal bunkers, are the only really water-tight portions of the ship. Whoever has gazed down into the capacious hold of such a steamer will readily understand that if the water should pour into one of these spaces, at either end of the ship, the other end of the vessel would rise steadily upwards. In nearly every case, even the largest steamer, just before sinking, tilts abruptly its bow or stern straight up out of the sea, until the water rushing into the hold draws the vessel downwards, and with a mighty roar it plunges forever into the deep. We have repeatedly noticed at this moment that the air within the boat escapes with a shrill whistle from every possible aperture, and the sound resembles the shriek of a steam siren. This is a wonderful spectacle to behold!

The velocity with which a ship sinks depends on the size of the hold, and its distance from the ship's center of gravity, for the suction occurs more rapidly if the ship is struck at either end than if the blow is delivered amidships.

We are seldom concerned with ships having empty holds; those we pursue usually carry heavy cargoes, and therefore the water can only penetrate within, where space and air exist; whatever air is left around loosely packed bales and boxes must be driven out before the water can stream in;

BRITISH HOSPITAL SHIP GLOUCESTER CASTLE, SHOWING RED CROSS ON BOW, SUNK IN THE
ENGLISH CHANNEL BY A GERMAN SUBMARINE

certain exceptional cargoes, like wool and cereals, absorb a given amount of water, but these can be discounted.

Accordingly the air must escape through existing holes, as the water pouring in drives the air into the hold; the pressure with which the water comes in is equal to the air pressure in the hold. It is quite conceivable that a cargo may be so closely packed that there will be no space léft for air to escape, but this is hardly ever the case; frequently, however, the cross-sections of the air vents are so small that the air escapes only very slowly, and the water enters very slowly in the same ratio; under these conditions it would take a long time for a ship to sink. This undoubtedly is very desirable in peace time, but in time of war this is not at all agreeable to our purpose; first, if the foundering of the vessel is prolonged we are prevented from accomplishing other work, and secondly, warships may come to the assistance of a sinking steamer.

Whenever possible we found it expedient to break open with an axe big holes in the lockers in case the hatch could not be quickly enough removed; or, if circumstances did not permit of our doing this, we shot holes with our cannon into the upper part of the steamer, above the hold, so that the air might conveniently escape and the water rush in. We employed, with excellent results, this method in the sinking of many steamers which otherwise would have settled too slowly.

It happens sometimes that a ship may carry a cargo that floats and that is not porous, such as wood. It is impossible to sink a vessel with such a cargo by admitting water into the hold. Shots therefore must be fired at the engine and boiler rooms to force this kind of a steamer to sink. In general this is a safe rule to follow, for these are always the most vulnerable portions of every heavily laden vessel, and this mode of attack is nearly invariably successful.

A warship is usually equipped with cross or lateral bulkheads, in addition to the longitudinal bulkhead that runs from stem to stern through the middle of the ship, dividing it into halves, and other bulkheads separate these two longitudinal sections into further subdivisions. With the exception of the great fast passenger steamers, these divisions by means of longitudinal bulkheads seldom exist on vessels of commerce, although exceptions are to be found.

The sinking of a steamer with a multitude of partitions is effected by its gradually listing more and more on the side in which the water is penetrating, until it capsizes completely and founders with the keel uppermost. A ship can also roll over on its side as it plunges downwards with stem or stern erect.

Theoretically a vessel might sink on a parallel keel, descending horizontally deeper and deeper into the sea; but it never occurs in reality. This hypothesis assumes that a ship has taken in at the bow exactly the same amount of water as at the stern, at exactly the same distance from the center of gravity; this, of course, is impossible; besides the holes through which the water is pouring in must also be at precisely the same level, or else the water pressure would be greater at one end than at the other, and the slightest alteration of level would occasion a greater intake of water and upset the equilibrium of the boat.

There is one other point I will touch upon; it has often been asserted, especially in romances of the ocean, that as a ship sinks the suction creates a tremendous whirlpool which engulfs all things in its vicinity. This statement is naturally very much exaggerated. People swimming about may be drawn down by the suction of the foundering ship, but in my opinion no lifeboat which is well manned is in danger of this whirlpool. Even old sailors, deluded by this 'superstition, have rowed away in haste from a sinking ship, when they might have stood by and saved many lives.

The question is now often being put, whether it will be possible to raise the vessels that have been sunk during the war. The raising of a ship depends above all upon whether the depth at which it lies is so great that it precludes the work of a diver.

I have already stated that the water pressure augments at the rate of one atmosphere (one kilogram to the square centimeter) to ten meters' increase of depth. If a diver working at ten meters' depth is under a pressure of one atmosphere, at fifty meters he will be under the tremendous pressure of five atmospheres. This is the greatest depth to which a diver can attain, and if by chance a diver has gone a few meters beyond fifty meters, no man to my knowledge has attained sixty meters. The work of divers at a depth of forty or fifty meters is even then not very effective, as they are unable to perform heavy tasks, nor can they remain more than half an hour at a time under such a pressure, and I am speaking now only of experts; therefore only light and easy work can be performed by most divers at a great depth and the appliance of ponderous chains for lifting purposes can only be accomplished under unusually favorable conditions. To raise any ship at a depth above thirty meters must be considered as a very efficient job, whereas if this is attempted at a depth below thirty meters it can be done only by salvage companies where neither unfavorable bottom obstacles nor currents intervene. A strong current renders a diver's work impossible, for it carries him off his feet.

On the high seas the currents change with the ebb and flood. At the precise moment of the turn of the tide the undercurrent is supposed to be nil, and the diver must take advantage of this moment to perform his task. Another difficulty arises from the sand being shifted by the currents, and settling on the prominent parts of a wreck; it often envelops them to such a degree that the ship becomes so deeply embedded in the sand that it is no longer salvable.

According to my estimation eighty per cent of our enemy's sunken ships lie from fifty to a hundred meters below the surface of the sea, so that all possibility of their being raised is excluded. The largest ships nowadays have a draft of less than ten meters, and as the vessels sunk lie at far greater depths they are no source of danger to shipping in time of peace. Of the remaining twenty per cent of sunken ships half of them are unreclaimable, either owing to their position, or owing to the high cost of salvage, or because it is not even known where they lie. The other half or last ten per cent have probably for the greater part been sunk in channels where the currents are so swift that they are covered with sand, and diving enterprises are out of the question. In time of war such work cannot be thought of; after the war the ships will long since have been completely buried by the sand.

Maybe off the east coast of England one or two ships may be raised, for they lie at a lesser depth and are exposed to slighter currents than on the south coast of England, but in that district only the smaller and more insignificant vessels have been sunk, and it would hardly pay to raise them, especially as they are so damaged by torpedoes and mines that they would probably fall apart on being raised to the surface.

Therefore hardly a single ship will be salvaged, and the sea will retain all those ships it has swallowed in the course of this war carried on by all the nations of the earth.

THE END

The Riverside Press
CAMBRIDGE . MASSACHUSETTS
U . S . A

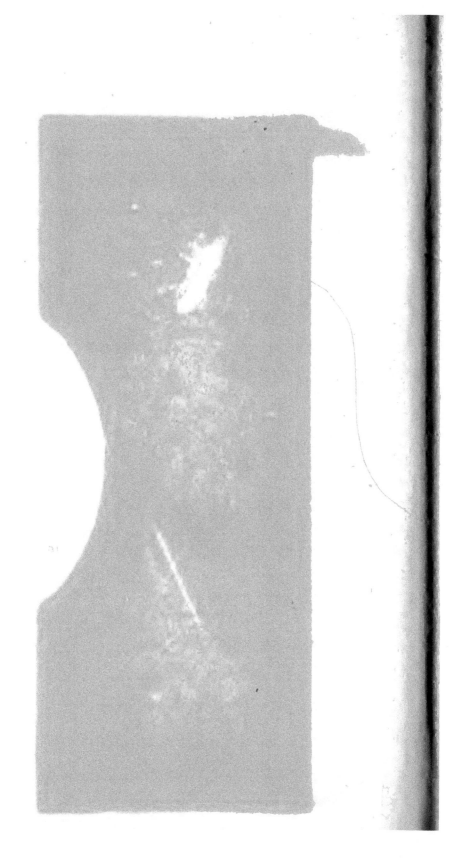